A Family

By Mary McKenna

A FAMILY
A Carillon Book

Carillon Books Edition published 1978
ISBN: 0-89310-029-3 (hardbound)
        0-89310-030-7 (paperback)
Library of Congress Catalog Card Number: 77-951-68
Copyright © 1978 by Carillon Books
Printed in the United States of America

Carillon Books
2115 Summit Avenue
St. Paul, Minnesota 55105 U.S.A.

To My Grandparents,
My Mother and Father,
To Pete,
Our Children, and
Our Children's Children

Acknowledgements

Scripture texts used in this work are taken from the NEW AMERICAN BIBLE, copyright © 1970, by the Confraternity of Christian Doctrine, Washington, D.C., and are used by permission of copyright owner. All rights reserved.

Prologue

My great-grandmother, my grandmother, and my mother were liberated before they knew the meaning of the word—they had minds of their own. I thought I had inherited this legacy, but there I sat, "barefoot, pregnant, and in the kitchen." I had shed my shoes which were two sizes too small for my swollen feet. For the ninth time in eleven years my tummy was ballooning like a mound of leavened bread dough, and I was gorging myself with homemade fudge. I had just come home from the obstetrician's office where I passed my routine check.

When Dr. McCaffrey examined me he usually had a stern, concerned look on his face that made his heavy black eyebrows almost meet over his nose. This time he smiled, "Mary, you were made to be a mother!" When you're lying on that narrow, stiff examining table with your legs dangling in the cold stirrups, your defenses are down. (I hear that now they first see you fully clothed in a consulting room, they cover the stirrups, and they warm the speculum.)

Jokingly for the past few years I had been offering him my very healthy uterus for a transplant. I was tired of hearing how strong my support muscles were and how I didn't have a stretch mark from all my pregnancies.

"But Doctor, I'm almost thirty-nine years old! I'll be sixty before this baby is through college!"

Dr. McCaffrey's dark eyes softened, "Mary, you'll be a young sixty!"

That was sixteen years ago, and I have been a mother almost 10,000 days, roughly half my life. In the total picture, there have been more good days than bad, more happy than sad, and I have been free to do the most important job in the world: procreate and nurture children.

Although "togetherness" was necessarily the trademark of our family when the children were growing up, I have tried to convey an awareness of each child's individuality and value.

Recently, I spent weeks cutting, pasting, and labeling snapshots, clippings, and mementoes to make a "This Is Your Life" book to give to our twenty-five-year-old daughter at her bridal shower. When our first three children were married, I had done the same thing for them, and they treasured their life stories as a personal gift from their father and me.

As I completed the album, our youngest daughter, number eight of our nine children, watched me with a sullen face.

"What's the matter, Nellie?" I asked. "Don't you like the book? Or is it the mess I'm making? I'll clean it up when I'm through."

She thought awhile, and then slowly muttered, "No, Mom, it's not either one. It's just that I'm afraid there won't be anything left when it's my turn to get a book. I don't think you have nine copies of anything!"

She was right. How could I continue this precedent without the material to work with?

A plaque on our bedroom wall gave me a clue. "There are only two lasting bequests we can give children—one is roots, the other, wings."

None of them had any difficulty with the wings; some even left the nest too soon. But roots I could give them.

My brothers and I had written the genealogy of our children's grand-, great-grand-, and great, great-grandparents so they were familiar with "the olden days." I wanted to tell them the story of their own family; the important and the insignificant things that we take for granted they know.

My resources were unlimited. We have over 3000 feet of home movies covering every major event in our family, beginning with our wedding. Besides the nine baby books I wrote in sporadically, we have nineteen photograph albums and enough loose pictures to fill numbers twenty and twenty-one. Since 1957, before Ann Landers said they were a "no, no", I have been writing Christmas letters to our friends and relatives in other parts of the country. Each year the story of our family unfolded. I have included in this book a few articles which I wrote for the *Catholic Digest* about our family life. For filling in long forgotten details, I had my husband's remarkable memory.

I have tried to recall the good times and the bad; but God, in His wisdom, has tempered my memory with a convenient forgetfulness. I remember mostly the good.

I would hope that our children might learn from this story of our family life to seize and appreciate the happy moments, and to accept and survive the crosses. These, too, shall pass.

Chapter I

The bridegroom beamed when he heard hushed whispers as his bride walked down the aisle with her father. Peter J. McKenna had never seen his bride in her wedding gown. In fact, he had never seen his bride.
—*The Washington D.C. Times Herald,* June, *1949.*

Our wedding day, June 9, 1949, was ideal. "Then, if ever, come perfect days," and we had one. There was a gentle breeze, temperature in the low eighties, a clear blue sky—everything my mother had prayed for.

Recently I realized what my mother had gone through twenty-eight years ago. When our daughter Margaret was married, our whole family was together again, a house full of adults. They had come from both coasts and Texas to share this happy time. Each meal was a boarding-house production, temporary beds were set up each night and dismantled each morning. It was work, but it was fun.

The preparations in that spring of 1949 had begun with a thorough house cleaning; each room had to look like a potential guest room. In Browerville, Minnesota, my mother couldn't reserve a hall, just our house and yard. She couldn't hire professional caterer, just loyal, hardworking women who exchanged these services. They came days ahead to bake the Polish coffee cakes. Pete and his relatives and friends also arrived days ahead from

Washington, D.C., and ate the poppy seed coffee cakes as fast as the women baked them. For three days before the wedding, my poor mother had to feed, entertain, and find rooms for these extra guests, plus having the turmoil of being the "mother of the bride." In a town of seven hundred people you couldn't make reservations at a Holiday Inn; your friends and neighbors had to help you out with guest rooms. And they did.

The wedding was a family affair. My brother, who had been ordained a priest in the Crosier Order three years before, offered the Solemn Nuptial High Mass with three other priests. Pete's only brother, Joe, couldn't come, so he chose his father as his best man. My sister Jackie was my maid of honor, and the rest of my family were involved as bridesmaids, ushers, and altar boys. My Aunt Rosie played the organ, and my Aunt Florence sang "Ave Maria" and "On This Day, O Beautiful Mother."

Father Dick read the awesome exhortation from the old Roman ritual:

> *This union then, is most serious, because it will bind you together for life in a relationship so close and so intimate that it will profoundly influence your whole future. That future, with its hopes and disappointments, its successes and its failures, its pleasures and its pains, its joys and its sorrows, is hidden from your eyes. You know that these elements are mingled in every life and are to be expected in your own. And so, not knowing what is before you, you take each other for better or for worse, for richer or for poorer, in sickness and in health, until death.*

With the beauty of the day, the joy of our love, and the excitement of sharing our wedding day with our family and friends, I had been up in the clouds. All at once as I listened to this realistic approach, I came back to earth. "Not knowing what is before you"—that was the smartest move God ever made. If I had known that in three days I'd be pregnant for the first of nine times, that I'd be washing diapers every other day for the next thirteen years, and that Pete would have to wait twenty-eight years to get his first professional job, I probably would have left him at the altar!

Thank the good Lord we were both blind on our wedding day.

Father Dick concluded with "What, therefore, God hath joined together—." This joining had started more than four years before, on April 2, 1945. I was in Minneapolis, Minnesota, and Pete was thousands of miles away in Kassel, Germany, but it was a circuitous part of God's plan for our lives.

I knew the path I had taken, but I had to talk to many people to get Pete's story—his mother, his chaplain, his hospital buddies, and of course, him. We had been married many years before he would talk freely about his blindness.

Chapter II

April 2, 1945. Minneapolis, Minnesota.

> KEEP CALM
>
> Student nurses
> are doing their
> best.

The sign hung in the busy pediatric ward of Minneapolis General Hospital. It had been put up as a joke, but it wasn't funny.

"Hey, Nurse, look what the Easter Bunny brought me!"

"Nurse, will you raise my bed so I can see out the window?"

"I dropped my drinking tube, Nurse, and it broke all over. Can I have another one?"

"All right, you guys, one at a time. I only have two hands, you know."

I stepped warily over the half-eaten jelly beans on the floor. Every holiday there was an overdose of treats, the rest of the time, famine. I balanced the breakfast tray with one hand as I cranked the head of the bed up, and then very carefully rested the tray over the child's knees.

"Here you are, Tim, orange slices, toast, and yummy cream of wheat. I'll put jelly on your toast for you."

The dry toast was one of the many curtailments of the war; butter was scarce for civilians.

I continued with each child's tray until they were all served. My motions were mechanical and my mind and heart didn't seem to be involved with what I was doing. I was still tired, and there is nothing as worn out as a worn out nurse!

It was my first day back from the Elizabeth Kenny Institute where I had spent the last few weeks wringing out woolen hot packs used on the polio patients. Just thinking about it brought back the smell of the hot wet wool. The packs were put on the paralyzed limbs to relax them before the technicians did the passive exercises to retrain the muscles. Sister Kenny's theories were widely accepted by this time, and along with most of the country, as a young nurse I was in awe of her. One day I was scurrying down the hall with a bedpan and Sister Kenny was approaching from the opposite direction. I jumped to the right to avoid bumping into her, but she moved to the right, too. Then we both side-stepped to the left. It was like a scene from Alfonse and Gaston; Sister Kenny, one hundred seventy-five pounds at five feet eight, and I, one hundred pounds at five feet nothing. As I dodged to the right, bedpan still intact, I detected a faint smile on the Australian woman's face.

It was Easter Monday, a chilly but sunny morning, and all of Minneapolis was alive with the promise of spring. It had been a long gray winter, and it had seemed to me that the war would go on forever. Yesterday had been the brightest Easter since the war began, even though the most popular hues in the Easter Parade remained olive drab and navy blue.

The Allied armies were converging from all directions and were within 150 miles of Berlin. They were taking thousands of Nazi prisoners, and, according to yesterday's headlines, General Eisenhower was giving Germany instructions on how to surrender. Just that morning the radio was braodcasting news of the Yanks going into Okinawa in the Pacific. V-E Day could be within the month! The fellows, including my brother Harry, would be coming back. Even more significant right now was that the nurses would return to the hospitals at home.

It wasn't easy being a student nurse during the war. Most of the "grads" had gone into the service so that after the six months' probation period, the students were working all three shifts and taking charge of the wards. Sixty hours a week of classes and duty were not unusual. After being at General Hospital only six weeks, as a new student nurse I was sent to work on "Station H", the N & M (Nervous and Mental) Ward. The ride up in the rattling cage that served as the elevator was a prelude to the scariness of that six-week stint. The first day the supervisor handed me a bunch of keys to let myself in and out of the rooms. Then she showed me around the ward where patients stared into nothingness or talked and laughed to themselves. Holding convulsive patients who were given insulin shock therapy was a scene I'd remember forever.

I barely survived the psychiatric training when I was sent to the OR (Operating Room). As the surgeon amputated a leg, I stood near the door trying to hold on to my queasy stomach. When the "float" nurse handed me the bucket with the severed leg, I could have quit nursing right then, the first of many times.

Each rotation was a challenge, from the preemie nursery where a new baby died in my arms, to the Contagion Ward where I caught the mumps, to the many months on the medical and surgical wards where the "poor and indigent" became real persons with whom to share love and concern.

There were 96,000 of us Cadet Nurses throughout the United States who had pledged "to do my duty for my country by service to my fellowmen for the duration plus six months—so help me God."

Even with the long hours, we students found time to play. We danced at the USO, had our own softball team, played tennis when we could wrangle the court away from the interns, and once in a while we splurged on a movie or a night at Harry Ware's Bar. Fifteen dollars a month plus streetcar tokens to get to classes at the University made for a slim budget. White stockings, cigarettes when they were available, and three-cent stamps gobbled up the monthly allowance. Oh, the postage! Most of the girls had long distance romances going, but they lost a lot of zing in a miniature photocopied V-Mail love letter. Our biggest sacrifice for the war effort, we thought, was the acute shortage of men. Dates were scarce.

Almost every night there was a sing-a-long in the nurses' dorm. "The Whiffenpoof Song", "Sentimental Journey", and "Oh, Johnny" were some of our favorites. We had our own version of "Ja Da":

> *General, General, listen while we sing to you.*
> *General, General, where the patients are never too few.*
> *If you're poor and indigent, too*
> *This here place is the place for you—oh*
> *General, General, Fifth Street and Sixth Avenue.*
> *We want your bo-dy—Fifth Street and Sixth Avenue.*

Victory-In-Europe Day came on May 8, and only three months later, on August 15, V-J Day. That evening the nurses' residence was empty; everyone had literally danced down the street to Nicollet Avenue to join the cheering, hugging, deliriously happy mob. THE WAR WAS OVER!

Slowly the RNs came back from the service and resumed their jobs at the "charge desks." We student nurses were relieved when we could hand over the responsibilities; we had learned much from the experience, but we were exhausted.

The last year of training was easier; being a senior meant fewer classes and more practical work, real bedside nursing on the medical and surgical floors. One Christmas Eve stands out in my mind when I had all the men tucked in for the night, and as a special treat, turned on the radio to listen to Christmas music. Suddenly I heard a loud sobbing from the corner bed in the ward.

"Why, Oscar, what's the matter? Don't you like the music?"

"Oh ya, I luv da musick, but it reminds me of my vife. She alwiss fixed me oyster stue on Christmas Eef."

Then there was the time the police brought in an eighty-nine-year-old man from his one-room flat; he was emaciated, crusted with dirt, and crawling with vermin. I asked them to put him directly into the bath tub. He was a real challenge. I scrubbed, deloused, shampooed, and manicured until he looked like a new man. When I finally tucked him into bed he looked so clean, comfortable and content, but just to make sure I asked, "Now, Henry, is there anything else you want before I leave?"

The octogenarian's eyes sparkled, he sat upright, grabbed me around the waist, and from his toothless mouth panted, "Yeah you!"

Finally, I spent three summer months of "Rural Nursing" on the shores of Lake Bemidji. People paid a good price to live in this vacationland, so, for the nurses who had spent the last three years in downtown Minneapolis, it was luxury. The swimming, the boating, and most of all the DATING, was a pleasant ending to my nurses' training.

Then it was over. Three years of long hours, night duty, emotional involvement with patients, fallen arches and varicose veins. I was marching through Memorial Field to a fast "Pomp and Circumstance" to pick up my diploma. A few months later my joy was complete; I had passed my state board examinations and was REGISTERED in the state of Minnesota. This was the time for me to decide what to do next; jobs were open everywhere.

The forty-one girls in our class had become close, and it was sad to see them go in every direction. It was their first going away, some to California, some to New Orleans, and others to Colorado. Because my brother Harry worked for the government, I chose to go to work at Mt. Alto Veterans' Hospital in Washington, D.C., and that made all the difference.

Chapter III

April 2, 1945. Kassel, Germany.

The floor was hard and dirty, but it was the best mattress the anti-tank squad of the 80th Infantry Division of Patton's Third Army had slept on in weeks. It had been a long, hard push through the Ruhr Basin, and now all the American, French, and British forces were converging to cut off the German supply line. They were within one hundred and fifty miles of Berlin.

Because they had been driving until midnight that night, the guard had to shake the squad leader, Peter McKenna, a twenty-year-old staff sergeant. He awoke slowly, remembering they had holed up in a deserted medical clinic—the surgical instruments, the examining tables, even the antiseptic smell was still there.

"Hey, Sarge, get up," the guard yelled at him. "A messenger just told me the Krauts are coming up from Kassel. 'Tiger Royal tanks,' he said. Y' better scout down the road and see."

"Huh? Uh, what time is it? Seems like I just sacked in."

"It's four-thirty. The sun'll be up in an hour. Here's your watch. Thanks for letting me use it."

It was the only watch in the squad so everyone used it on guard duty. It had been a gift from Pete's parents when he went into the army two and a half years earlier. He slipped the watch into the side of his boot and started out on his scouting mission.

There was a heavy row of bushes along the sides of the road and tall trees obstructed the view beyond them. Pete had to walk to a clearing at the top of the hill about a half mile away from where he and his squad had made camp. He could see the still sleeping city of Kassel sprawled out below him. A railroad tunnel crossed the road at the bottom of the long hill.

"We'll fire at them as they come through the tunnel," he thought. "It's the only way they can come."

As he turned to go back and put his strategy into effect, he spotted them. They had already come through the tunnel and were spreading out from the bottom of the hill—about a half dozen sixty-ton tanks and a couple dozen riflemen. In a few minutes he'd be surrounded, so he crept back into the bushes. As he knelt in the thicket, he prayed to God his men would be aware of their approach. In a matter of minutes he had an answer; he heard firing from his anti-tank squad. The blasts came with such force that he was sure all the Germans had retreated to the bottom of the hill.

When the firing stopped, Pete went back onto the road toward his camp. He had gone a few hundred feet when he found an anti-tank gun his men had left behind. He aimed it at the retreating tanks.

"Now, if I can hit those Krauts, we'll blast that tunnel and capture the whole bunch."

His one-man assault was being watched, though, by one German tank still up on the hill. As he was loading his 57 mm tank shell, the German tank gunner let go of a powerful 88 mm tank shell. Fragments of it hit the shell Pete was loading and they both exploded in his face. The American colonel who was in charge of the battalion found Pete a short time later, lying unconscious beside his gun. The officer sent his driver back for aid and went on his way to assess the enemy's new position. Before the jeep came with a stretcher, Pete had regained consciousness. He was numb. "My God, what happened?"

He could feel blood oozing from his face, but when he tried to touch it he couldn't move his arms; his left hand was limp.

"My arms! I can't move them. They must be broken!" He tried to focus his eyes. "Oh, no—dear God, I can't see anything!"

He knew if he stayed there he might bleed to death. He tried to raise himself, but couldn't support himself with his arms. He finally pushed himself up against a small tree until he was on his feet. Then he limped slowly, sightlessly, back on to the road, listening for noises. He was sure he was walking away from the ill-fated hill. He figured if he kept one foot on the blacktop and the other on the gravel shoulder, he'd eventually get back to his camp. This was his first lesson in orientation.

When the men in his squad saw him staggering up the road, they rushed to help him. "What in God's name hit you, Mac?" his corporal asked as he laid him down on a tarp. They cleaned some of the blood off and applied pressure to stop the bleeding. "My foot," he mumbled, "take off my boot." As they tugged at the dirty, blood-encrusted boot, the watch his parents had given him fell out. He'd been walking on it. His buddy, Charlie Miller, offered it to him. "You keep it, Charlie, I don't think I'll need it any more." He lapsed into unconsciousness again.

Two medics laid Pete in the stretcher and attached it to the hood of the jeep. It was a bumpy ten miles to the field hospital; the wind blowing on his face seemed to expose jagged nerve endings. He moaned. The medic held a towel over his head to shield it.

Pete was unconscious most of the way to the big tent hospital. As soon as he arrived, the Catholic chaplain gave him the last rites of the Church. He could hear part of what the priest was saying, "By this holy annointing . . . may the Lord forgive . . . wrong you have done by . . . sight . . . hearing . . . touch . . ."

"My sight? My touch? What have I done, Father?"

Then the priest gave him the viaticum, "Receive, my brother, this food for your journey, the Body of our Lord Jesus Christ, that He may guard you from the malicious enemy and lead you into everlasting life."

"Am I dying, Father?"

"No, son, we're asking for the healing power of God, His presence, for you."

"He must still want me around, Father, but I don't know what for. I CAN'T SEE! Won't I ever see?"

The field doctor made a cursory diagnosis: face shot off, both arms fractured, left hand mutilated with thumb and forefinger dangling, both eyes gone. Even in his semi-delirious condition

Pete realized the extent of his injuries. He had heard the doctor's words "optic nerves are damaged" and "better do an enuclea-tion." Even before they told him, he knew he was blind.

"Oh, God," he thought, "why me? I'm only twenty years old! I've got my whole life ahead of me. I love being a soldier—wanted to stay in—" He drifted out again. The numbness had gone, and the pain was excruciating as they set his arms, dressed his empty eye sockets, and amputated his dangling fingers.

During the ambulance ride from the field hospital to Mainz, Pete went in and out of consciousness again. He was aware of a long pontoon ride over the Rhine River, but mostly it was a blur. When he awoke, he was being loaded onto an airplane, and under the bandages on his face he tried to smile. "Hey, this is my very first plane ride!" They flew him from Mainz to Rheims where he stayed a few days before he was put on a train to Paris. The first time he became aware of what day it was—up to now days and nights had been indistinguishable—he was in a hospital ward in Paris. All the patients and hospital personnel seemed to be griev-ing. The fellow in the next bed told him bluntly that Franklin Roosevelt was dead. It was the twelfth of April. Their "father figure" was gone.

Three days later, Pete was put on another plane bound for the states. At their first stop, the Azores, the medics took all the patients off the plane and placed their stretchers under the wing to shade them from the hot sun. While the crew refueled and re-stocked medical supplies, the nurses passed out refreshments. One of them held a drinking tube through the hole in his dressing so he could sip some cool pop.

"Mmmm, good!" he mumbled between sucks on the straw. "Sure wish I could use my hands. Thanks a lot, nurse."

This scene was repeated when they reached Bermuda.

On April 18, Pete entered the hospital at Mitchell Air Force Base near New York where doctors decided where each patient would be sent for treatment. Each new patient was allowed a long distance call, courtesy of the telephone company. An orderly wheeled the portable phone to Pete's bed. "Pete, here's the tele-phone. If you want to call your parents, I'll dial the operator for you. There you go, the phone is right by your mouth."

So many times in the last two weeks he had wished he could have talked to his mother and dad. It would have been a lot easier if they had just been near him. They had always been a close family. "Mom! This is Pete!"

"Thanks be to God, Junior! Pop, it's Junior on the line! Are you all right?" She was crying.

"I'm gonna be okay, Mom." He was crying.

"Was it bad, son? The telegram from the War Department didn't say much—we regret to inform you—you know. It didn't give any specifics."

"At least I'm alive and back in the states, Mom. That's good, isn't it?"

"Is it ever! I'm so thankful. Was it bad?"

"Mom, it's good to hear your voice." He was on the verge of tears again. "Where's Dad?"

"He's right here. Go ahead, Pop. Ask him when we can see him."

"Dad? Gosh, you sound great! Say, Dad, ah—I'm shot up pretty bad."

"Oh, no! What—?" He heard his father start to ask.

"You better prepare Mom before she comes up here. Tell her I'll be all right, though. The doctors said you could come up here anytime."

"Here's your mother again."

"Thanks for calling, darling. We'll see you real soon. God love you, Junior. Goodbye!"

The next day they took the train to New York.

The doctors decided that Pete should go to Dibble Hospital in California, but they hadn't reckoned with the iron hand of his Irish mother. Why should her son be sent across the country where they wouldn't be able to visit him? She contacted a man she knew in the Surgeon General's Office in Washington. He ate at the cafeteria where she worked during the war. The Army changed its plans! Pete was sent to Valley Forge General Hospital in Phoenixville, Pennsylvania, instead—only a three hour drive from Washington. His mother and father visited him every week. On Sunday morning they would go to mass at six o'clock in the morning and then start their pilgrimage to his bedside. It was only after Pete's arrival at Valley Forge that his parents learned what was beneath his bandages. The doctors here told them their son was blind. It seemed easier for them to accept than the telegram from the War Department.

The year before, on Mother's Day in 1944, Pete and his mother had posed for a picture for the Washington newspaper when he arrived at Union Station. Everyone who saw the picture thought Pete was a handsome fellow—deep grey eyes, long black eyelashes, and a strong, Adonis-like perfectly shaped nose and mouth. Now the doctors were using the picture just as an orthopedic doctor would use an X-ray. Maybe it was a blessing Pete couldn't look into a mirror; he needed a nose, lips, eyelids, eyebrows, and new facial tissue. For one year the plastic surgeon rebuilt Pete's face.

At the same time that they were rebuilding his face, Pete was rebuilding his morale with the help of the hospital chaplain, Father Murphy, and his own deep faith in God. They had many long talks in the first few months. Pete was convinced that it was the healing power of Jesus that helped him accept his blindness.

"But aren't you bitter, Pete?" Father Murphy asked him a few weeks after he had been admitted to the hospital.

"I sure was at first, Father. But since I've talked to the other blind guys in this ward, I consider myself pretty lucky."

"Why's that, Pete?"

"Some of them don't have anybody—no one who cares. I've got my family. Take that fellow in the corner, f'r instance," he lowered his voice, "his wife is divorcing him. He's—gee—he's hopeless. He doesn't even believe in God. Thank God, I do. I may be blind but my life was spared for some good reason."

"You're a lucky guy, Pete, to have such faith."

"You've helped me a lot, Father."

"I hope I've helped you a little, cause you've helped me a lot."

Pete had a healthy self-image and was optimistic about his future. He learned his way around the ward and visited with other men who had similar injuries. He spent hours swapping war stories with them. Take Don Weeks who was in the 80th Division with him. One day when he was looking for land mines in the Moselle River, he found one with his pole and it blew up in his face. Another fellow, Bill Keefe, was a medic in a hospital. When he was washing windows in the ward one day a bomb hit and shattered glass in his face.

One day, his old friend Charlie Miller came to Valley Forge Hospital to visit Pete, bringing with him the watch Pete had in his boot when he was injured. Charlie had made such a pilgrimage out of his visit that Pete had to take the watch back, even though he had no use for it. Later he gave it to his younger brother, Joe. The American Foundation for the Blind had given Pete a Braille watch and he had mastered reading the dots on the dial.

When his scars healed, Pete went up to Avon, Connecticut, for orientation and rehabilitation into his new life of blindness. The government had taken over the campus of a boys' school to train the newly-blinded veterans in the ways of living. They used novel and progressive ideas in their approach to blindness.

At Valley Forge Pete had learned the Hoover cane technique—swinging a long white cane from side to side and literally clearing a path ahead of him. At Avon, they took their canes away, except when they were off campus. With three hundred blind men waving their canes, it would have been an en masse duel! Pete learned to use sounds and the feel of the wind and sun on his face to detect when he was approaching objects. He learned how to walk up and down stairs safely—even how to fall down the right way.

In four and a half months he learned to be completely mobile and to travel independently. He learned the proper way to eat, shave, take care of his wardrobe, go into town to shop, and to spend and keep track of his money. For his future use in learning a trade or going to school, he learned Braille, typing, how to use manual and electric tools, how to use a potter's wheel, and how to operate a vending stand. The men were given psychological and vocational counseling so that they could get back into the mainstream of society with a positive attitude.

After another six months at Valley Forge Hospital to graft a pedicle of skin from his stomach to his injured left hand, Pete was ready to get on with living. He went back home to Washington, D.C. The Veterans Administration offered him more counseling to decide what he should do with his life. Pete was interested in

working with other blind or handicapped people, but he realized
that he would need more education and training. He took more
Braille and typing courses through the School for the Blind in
Washington, and in September, 1947, he enrolled at Catholic University. His father worked at the Soldiers' Home near the campus, so he drove Pete to school each day. Ira Riggles of the V.A.
had given him a complete orientation of the campus, and from
then on he found his own way to his classes. The university gave
him a study room to use with his readers who were provided by
the Veterans Administration. He took a full load of courses, and
he proved to himself, his family, and the V.A. that he could return
to a normal college life.

When school was out in June, he returned to Mt. Alto Veterans'
Hospital in Washington for more plastic surgery on his neck. That
move made all the difference.

Chapter IV

I liked working the evening shift, especially in the spring. Washington was in bloom from early March, and my mornings were free to enjoy its beauty. I rented a bicycle to ride through Rock Creek Park, strolled down Massachusetts Avenue, wondering about the strange foreigners who lived in the big embassies, and enjoyed the antics of the baboons and bears at the zoo. By mid-afternoon I didn't mind going to work.

It was the eighteenth of June, and when I received the report from the "day" nurse, she mentioned that one of the new patients, Peter McKenna, was blind. "But he takes care of himself," she added quickly, when she noticed my questioning glance.

I didn't give him much more thought as I got into the evening routine—four o'clock meds, pre-op orders, and a few I.V.'s to check. As I was charting at my desk after supper, I heard a tap, tap, tap along the corridor and finally I saw the tip of a white cane at my office door. I jumped up and blurted something about being "sorry I forgot to come and help you eat."

He laughed, "I managed, thank you. Say, what's your name? I hate calling everyone nurse. Each one of you sounds different, and I like your voice."

"I'm Miss John," I said loudly. "Can I help you with anything?"

"No, I'm just out for a walk. Have to see what's going on." A

blind man out for a walk? To *see* what was going on? My mind
wandered back to a cold Saturday night in Minnesota about ten
years before. It had been clear and cold as I had gone out the back
door of our home, and I was anxious to meet the gang at Dan's
Cafe. Saturday nights were alive in a small town; all the stores
were open, the theater was usually packed, and the juke boxes
went wild. The moonlight on the snow destroyed the darkness,
but something sounded eerie in our back yard. I listened. Was it a
cat or a dog moaning? I listened again.

"Yesus, Maria!—Yesus, Maria!" It was our eighty-year-old
Polish neighbor, Mr. Schenk. All he had on was his long winter
underwear as he crawled along the fence in the snow. He couldn't
see and he was lost. That had been my only experience with a
blind person, and now I didn't know how to treat this one.

Would he be safe in the halls? Would he fall down the open
stairs? How would he find his way back to bed? I needn't have
worried. Pete had been a patient on the ward before and knew his
way around. He visited with other patients and was less bother
than the men with perfect vision. When I moistened the dressings on his neck where he'd had plastic surgery, I tried very
hard to treat him with the cool compassion a young nurse
develops. But he intrigued me; he was totally blind, his face was
disfigured, he had two fingers missing, and he was making jokes!

When I came to work the next afternoon, Pete had learned my
name. While I was moistening his dressings, he mused, "Mary
John, that's a nice name. You know, Mary, I'm doing some research for my psych class at Catholic U. Would you be one of my
subjects?"

I had heard lots of lines from my patients, but never this one.
"You want me to be a statistic?" I joked facetiously.

"Just write your name, address, and telephone number on this
paper. I'll explain the research to you some other time."

I forgot all my defenses and gave him the information.

Each day that Pete was on the ward I found a certain excitement about going to work. One day, the old man in the bed next
to his said, "You know, Pete, Miss John's the only nurse whose
seams are straight in her white stockings!" That started an embarrassing repartee.

"You'll just have to take his word for it, Pete. I'm not about to let you Braille my legs!"

The end of the second week Pete went out on a weekend pass and early Saturday morning my phone rang. "Mary, this is Pete . . . how would you like to go out with me tonight? I checked and I know you're off duty."

"Huh, Pete? Who? How did you know where? Who gave you my number?"

"You did, Dummy. You're the only 'subject' in my research data!"

Our first date was on July 15, 1948. Pete came to my apartment building with his brother, Joe, and Joe's fiancee, Alma—neither of whom had met me. When they asked for Miss John, the receptionist sent them down to a Miss Johns who lived with four other girls. They went in, introduced themselves, had a cigarette, and listened to some records—thinking I was in the bedroom putting the finishing touches on my face. Finally, Miss Johns appeared.

"If you people are trying to sell something, I'm not interested."

Pete was the first one to catch the mistake. "You're not Mary John, are you? You don't sound like her."

Miss Johns directed them to Miss John's apartment, and we were on our way. After eating, dancing, and a very full evening, we made a date for the following week. I couldn't believe that he was blind; we went horseback riding, dancing, night clubbing, to the theater—just like any other couple. And he was such fun to be with.

We never discussed his blindness, but one Sunday afternoon I learned how sensitive he was about it. His parents had driven us to Chesapeake Bay for a picnic at their friends' cabin. About mid-afternoon, I hadn't noticed Pete was gone until I heard him call for his dad. He was in the bathroom. His dad went in and in a few minutes called for his brother, Joe. They gave no explanations when Joe came out, found a wrench, and went back to the bathroom. Then they asked for a first aid kit! I was getting more curious every minute. Finally, Pete emerged, noticeably embarrassed, with a patch over one eye—he had dropped his plastic eye down the drain and it was gone forever.

Mostly we ignored his "condition," as we referred to his blindness, and we continued dating through the summer. Before school started in September, Pete came back to the hospital for some minor plastic surgery, and by this time he was smitten by this nurse, and she was becoming fond of him, too. His proposals were becoming more frequent and more clever each week, but when he went public, I knew he was not handing me his usual Irish blarney.

It was show time at Mt. Alto Hospital, and I had brought the patients to the auditorium for their weekly entertainment by local groups. Some were on stretchers, some in wheelchairs, and some on crutches. Pete was the only one who came with a white cane. He found me and sat down. "Miss John, did you know the Kitchen Band from my mother's church is putting on the show tonight?"

"Yes, I heard that, Pete. You don't have to call me 'Miss John' just because I'm on duty."

"Wait'll you hear the song one of the women wrote. It's for you."

I didn't have to wait very long. After the opening number with the pots, pans, drums, and kazoos, I heard, "And now, one of your patients is going to sing a song dedicated to one of your nurses."

Pete was guided to the stage, and with more ardor than talent I heard "our song" for the first time.

> *Mary, I love you*
> *Say that you'll be true;*
> *Tell me you love me*
> *And no one else will do.*
> *When we are married*
> *How happy I will be,*
> *Then I'll have you and you'll have me.*
> *Mary, I love you.*

The whole auditorium was alive with the infectiousness of his love. He called me to the stage, and as I planted a kiss on his lips, the audience applauded. He knocked my stiff nurse's cap off my head as he tried for an encore. It was completely unrehearsed!

He knew my weakness; songs have been an important part of my life since the days when my mother sang us the songs that her mother had taught her. One, in particular, was written about my grandmother who was not known for her skill with pastry.

CAKE

Chorus: *C-A-K-E, that spells cake*
Just like mother used to make.
It was heavier than lead

Half a pound would kill you dead
Of the C-A-K-E mother used to make.

When Mother used to make a cake
Us boys would gather round
And holler till she gave us the pan to lick

Although she never left enough
For us to quarrel about

It always, always made us sick.
Repeat Chorus.

In my mother's musical family, before the invasion of the Victrola, the piano was the focal point of every family gathering. Every day after dinner one or the other of her sisters would go to the piano, instead of the dishpan, and play their old family favorites. For the liberated woman of the early 1900s they sang:

MOVIE SHOWS

Since Mother goes
To the movie shows,
Everything is on the blink,
Dirty dishes in the sink.
Since Mother goes
To the movie shows
Oh, the kitchen's some disgrace
And the ice box out of place.
How we miss her

We have no sister
And how we get along
Nobody knows.
We eat potato skins
Daddy props his pants with pins
Since Mother goes
To the movie shows!

My family has paraphrased this song many times. "When Mother writes, The family fights" or "When Mother skis, We're on our knees."

Another popular song during our courtship was "There's a Chapter in My Life Called Mary" and Pete wanted me to expand it into a whole book! As he talked of our getting married and moving to Minnesota, he sang the "Minnesota Rouser", "With Someone Like You, A Pal Good and True", and "The West, A Nest, and You, Dear." He knew where I was vulnerable.

Chapter V

A steady diet of the movies and radio shows of the thirties must have turned me into a romantic idealist, although during the serious days of the Depression my family didn't gush with endearing terms and touches. In fact, one night in particular, I remember my brother and I exposed a new and tender side of my quiet, reserved father.

Nothing had been different at the supper table that night. My dad always put cream and two spoons of sugar in his coffee and stir-r-red it while we all came to the table. Eight or nine heads bowed for a fast "Bless us, O Lord", and then everyone ATE. There was not too much conversation until the food was gone.

I had looked at my dad and felt a little guilty. My brother Harry and I had spent the afternoon in a little cubby hole behind the bathroom looking through an old trunk. There was a pack of letters tied with an old shoe lace, my mother's maiden name in faded pencil. At first the old two-cent stamps thrilled us most because we were into stamp collecting, and this was like finding a hidden treasure. Then, slowly and somewhat guiltily, we took the folded letters out of the envelopes and read the most romantic love letters we had ever seen.

"He must've copied this gooey stuff from a book," my brother said disgustedly. "How come he never talks like this now?" I thought the letters were beautiful.

"Daddy", I'd hesitated, "ah, how come your life was unbearable until a precious little red-head came into it? . . . The dearest, sweetest little girl in the world!''

He had looked at me as though I were speaking a foreign language. Finally I had to tell him what we'd found, and cruel as kids can be, my brother and I quoted some of the choicest and most intimate lines. He was embarrassed, but he didn't stop us. My mother seemed to enjoy them like a pleasurable memory. Afterward, we felt as though we had intruded into a private part of our parents' lives, but it gave us a new insight into my dad's real feelings. He was raised in a home where you never let them show, and he was able to write them much easier than to verbalize them. I have inherited some of this reticence.

Pete, on the other hand, was raised in an atmosphere of "honey, dear, and darling" and was much more adept at the language of the heart. When he was interviewed by the *Washington Star,* he called me the "Darling of Mt. Alto." I had never been called darling anything before. In my scrapbook of our first years, I have the cards that came with bouquets of flowers or boxes of candy—each one in different handwriting, but definitely Pete's thoughts. "Mary, it's a long time from Sunday till Wednesday"; "To my sweetheart, all my love, always"; "Mary, it's a dark day for the Republicans (Dewey, 1948!), but dinner Friday night will lighten things up a bit"; "Can you meet me at the University? Love, Pete"; "With all my love on your last day" (working at the hospital); and "Not quite an old married man yet! Love, Pete."

After six months of exciting and unusual dating, I realized that the fun and romance was turning into love and commitment. I wasn't ready for that.

One night as we sat in the car outside my apartment, Pete proposed again. He was becoming more insistent, while I was trying to dissuade him. "Let's both try dating other people, Pete. I like you an awful lot, but I just don't feel that I'm ready, or even willing for that matter, to marry you." Then I thought to myself, "Gee, that sounds cruel. Why did I ever let myself get so involved? Why did he get so serious? I'm just not big enough to be a blind man's wife. I'll just have to hurt Pete and cut off our relationship right now."

He wouldn't listen to my misgivings. "Don't you see, Mary,

(my spine tingled when he asked me that) if we love each other we can lick any problems we might have. What d'ya say, sweetheart?''

I must be firm or he's going to weaken me, I thought. ''I don't want to see you any more, Pete. I'll bring your car and anything else I have of yours and meet you at your classroom. Joe can drive you home.''

When we met at the University, I had a tight feeling in my stomach, my head ached, and my heart pounded. Thank goodness he couldn't see the hurt in my eyes as I handed him the car keys, the Trifari earrings, and the music box that played ''Stardust.''

''I don't want any of these reminders,'' he said, as he pushed the treasures aside. ''In fact, here's the rest of the jewelry I bought for you to match the earrings. You might as well have it. I'll never give it to anyone else.'' And then, almost as an afterthought, ''Say, how about dinner one more time as long as you're here?''

We drove to our favorite restaurant, had a cocktail, a long dinner, and serious conversation. ''Mary, do you love me?'' Pete asked, his artificial eyes glistening with real tears. I have always been able to communicate with my eyes and that was an aspect of our relationship that I missed. Now he seemed to be looking right at me, and I couldn't avert his eyes.

''Yes, I do, Pete, but . . .''

''That's all that's important, Mary. Don't you know that?''

''Yes,'' I sighed, ''I guess I do. I'm just—I'm just not sure. It seems like I should say yes, but I just don't know.''

''You don't have to make up your mind tonight, sweetheart. I can wait a long time if I have to.''

Through my tears, I promised, ''Pete, I'll pray about it and have an answer for you soon.''

From my Irish mother, I had learned that you sprinkled holy water to protect yourself in a storm. You made three wishes when you went into a church for the first time. Whenever you lost something, you said, ''Good St. Anthony, look around, something's lost and must be found.'' And on March 25, the feast of the Annunciation, you said a thousand Hail Marys and your prayers were always answered. With this child-like, or childish, faith I suggested that we attend the novena at his church—nine days of prayer before the feast of the Immaculate Conception.

On the second day of the novena, November 30, we had lunch downtown at the Cafe of Nations, and then Pete said, "How about a stroll down F Street? We can window shop."

As we walked along, I described the Christmas displays in each window, and suddenly we stopped. Pete knew downtown Washington better than I did, and he ushered me into Swope's Jewelry Store where a friend of his worked. "God, you're rushing me," I thought, "we're not finished with the novena yet!"

Twenty minutes later, I had the most beautiful diamond in the store, and, ready or not, we were engaged! The next seven days were prayers of thanksgiving for opening my eyes and heart to a love that was possible in spite of handicaps—which were mostly mine.

In 1948 kids didn't call home long distance; you wrote a letter and mailed it with a five-cent stamp. Our news was too good to go that slow route, and Pete insisted we call my parents the same night we became engaged. He always did things in an exciting, though not necessarily economical, way. We flew home to Minnesota during his Christmas vacation, so he could meet my family. When my father met us at the airport, he cried, and in my ecstatic state, I thought they were tears of happiness because his twenty-five-year-old daughter wouldn't have to go through life as a spinster. I didn't realize that Pete's scarred face would be a shock to people; I didn't notice it any more. Neither would my father or anyone else after they got to know him. Pete had won my father over by the time he drove us home to Browerville.

My teetotaling mother was enamoured by my Irishman, and woke him up each morning with a wee drop o' the grog to thaw out his bones on a cold Minnesota day. I think his visit awakened memories of almost thirty years before when she arrived, like Sinclair Lewis's Carol Kennicott in *Main Street,* in this little prairie village one hundred and fifty miles from her home in Minneapolis. She had come as a nineteen-year-old, only five feet tall, with flaming red hair, to teach English to second generation Poles and Germans. She had been used to challenge; at the University of Minnesota she'd been the goalie on the women's hockey team!

In her first months of teaching, she'd met my father who worked in the bank, and despite the tears and protests of her father, they were married and "settled" in Browerville. Unlike Carol Kennicott, my mother did not feel like "the educated young housewife trapped in a small town on the plains." She became absorbed with raising our family, six little Irish Polacks, plus a niece. Although there were only two other Irishmen in town, she didn't let us forget our heritage.

Pete and I set the date for our wedding, June 9, and I promised him that the deep snow would be gone by then.

Chapter VI

January 20, 1949, was a memorable day for at least three people in Washington: Pete, me, and Harry Truman. It was a cold, damp day for the Inauguration, but our spirits were high. I had a ticket to sit along Pennsylvania Avenue to view the parade, and Pete was going to be in it! I knew I'd have to leave early to go on duty at three o'clock so I sat on the north side of the street close to the bus line.

I was thrilled to see the President of the United States ride by with all the fanfare; even the other dignitaries were exciting, but my eyes kept straining ahead for the car of the blinded veterans in which Pete would be riding. After two hours I had to leave.

As soon as I got the report from the day nurse I rushed to Colonel McKeever's room. He was the only patient who had a television set—a four- by six-inch screen. In between passing medications and answering lights, I hovered over the tiny screen watching for Pete. Finally, the car went by in a flash; early television did not pan the scene or do instant replays. What a disappointment!

About an hour later, as I was serving the supper trays, I saw a soldier in full uniform coming down the hall. Then I saw the white cane. "Pete! What are you doing here? I just barely saw you on television!"

"I was afraid you'd missed the end of the parade. I wanted you to see me in my uniform 'cause a few more pounds and I'll never get into it again!"

Spring has always been a happy, hopeful time for me, and I think this feeling started with my second spring in Washington. Pete and I spent as much time together as we could between his classes and my work. We enjoyed each bit of new life, and it was especially thrilling for a Minnesotan to see buds opening up in late March. The cherry blossoms were something I'd read about, but we walked the paths along the Potomac and actually felt this early spring treat. I had never seen azaleas growing outside before. (Now twenty-eight years later I have a hardy one in my yard that has withstood our Minnesota climate. It is an annual reminder of our first spring in Washington.) As John Keats wrote, "A thing of beauty is a joy forever, Its loveliness increases, It will never pass into nothingness." When you share your eyes with someone you love, all the world looks good to you.

We shared more than the beauty of nature; we shared our time and friends and laughter. Sometimes we had to fit our dates into my strange hours at the hospital. On Ascension Thursday, before evening masses were allowed, I had to get to church at six o'clock in the morning. I was nonplussed when Pete asked if he could go with me. It meant an early taxi ride from southeast to northwest Washington, but if he wanted to go to all that effort to spend forty-five minutes with me at mass, I couldn't say no.

He arrived at my apartment building, the Chancery, at five-thirty. It was too early to meet me, so Bill, the night attendant, suggested that he wait in the lobby. He found a bench and had barely lit a cigarette when he heard a male voice asking, "Say, Buddy, would you do me a favor and hold my tripod on the roof? It's pretty windy up there, and I want to get a good shot of the sunrise."

Impulsively, Pete jumped up, left his cane behind on the floor, and volunteered, "Sure, be glad to." It had been a few years since he'd been aware of sunrises.

He followed closely behind the stranger—the noise from his rattling equipment was like Hansel and Gretel's pebbles helping Pete find his way—into the elevator, up eight flights, and out the door to the roof. "Let's leave this case in the doorway, so we won't get locked out," the photographer suggested as he left the door ajar.

Pete held the tripod steady while the man took several shots at different speeds and settings. It must have been a beautiful scene—the sun rising over the Gothic spires of the National Cathedral across the street and shining through the trees along Massachusetts Avenue.

With his mission completed, the man thanked Pete for his help, gathered up his camera equipment, repacked his tripod, and disappeared through the door.

When Pete heard the door shut, he knew he was in trouble. He called out, but the man was gone. He stood still for a few minutes wondering what he should do. The few traffic noises all seemed to be coming from one direction. He started to walk toward the sound, but he didn't know if there were a railing around the edge of the roof. "Better get on my knees," he thought, "so I won't fall overboard." He crouched down and made a circumference around him with his hands. It was gravel on tar and not too pleasant to kneel on, but he crept slowly toward the street side of the building. When he came to the edge he found the bricks were built up two or three feet, and he could stand up and wave over the ledge. He waved. He yelled. He stamped his feet. Hardly anyone in Washington who isn't a bird watcher, or sunrise enthusiast, is up before six o'clock in the morning, but he thought he could attract someone's attention on the eighth floor. Or maybe someone on the street. He did.

In ten minutes, the police were filling the lobby, the firemen were holding nets, and the tenants were outside waiting for the man to jump off the roof.

In the meantime back at the desk, Bill called my apartment to see if Pete had stopped off on the third floor to pick me up. When I said I hadn't heard from him, Bill knew what had happened. He slipped over to the elevator, went up to the roof, rescued Pete and brought him to my apartment, and went back to his desk. He didn't say a word to the anxious crowd until after Pete and I had strode through the lobby with our heads held high, looking very unconcerned and uninvolved with the commotion.

When we finally got to mass, a little late, we were both struck by the ridiculousness of the situation. Only God knew why we were convulsing with suppressed laughter.

Chapter VII

The month of April was busy and happy with bridal showers and going-away parties. I had selected my bridal gown and trousseau, and it was time for me to go home to Minnesota to Browerville, the small town I had left nine years earlier. I was going to be married in the same church in which I had been baptized, received my First Communion, and been confirmed.

I left Washington the second week of May. It was a sad farewell at Union Station when Pete came to say goodbye. Trains always seemed to be taking me away—first from Minnesota and now from Washington. They took the soldiers away during the war; I never remembered arrivals. We hated to think of being apart for a month, but thank God, we would both be busy.

When I got home, I had planned to surprise Pete by writing to him in Braille. I had a copy of the alphabet from the Library of Congress and I "borrowed" a slate and stylus from his desk at home. I started from the right hand side of the paper and laboriously punched out my message—one letter at a time.

He was surprised, but not as surprised as I was when I got his answer in Braille! He thought I knew how to read it, too. I had to turn it over and again very laboriously translate each cell:

My dearest darling,

What a pleasure it

was to receive a

letter from you in

such fine Braille

Is there no end of

the amazing things

you can do ?

After my surprise backfired, I wrote letters "to whom it may concern", not knowing who would read them to him. Pete typed his letters to me. We didn't need to have a hot love affair by correspondence because in a few weeks we'd be together for good.

Pete was busy with exams at school and coordinating the exodus from Washington to Browerville. His parents, his aunt, his friend, my brother, my roommate, and three of his mother's friends were all planning to be at our wedding. The caravan consisted of three cars; Pete's would be left with us in Minnesota.

They left Washington a week before the wedding and two and a half days later they all converged on my aunt in Minneapolis. She wasn't home when they arrived, but they went in and made themselves at home—all ten of them. When Aunt Rosie walked into her house a while later her guests were cooking, taking baths, and enjoying her hospitality. Pete's people were my relatives' kind of people.

Every family should have an Aunt Rosie. My earliest recollection of her was hearing my mother tell about her sisters, Agnes and Rosehelen, who ignored "proper conduct" for young ladies and hitchhiked from St. Cloud, where they went to Normal School, to Browerville back in 1921. After seventy miles in Model T cars and dusty roads, they were so disheveled that my mother wanted to disown them. She was only a year older than they, but marriage and a baby had begun to turn her into a proper small-town matron.

When Aunt Rosie finished college and went up to Warroad, Minnesota, near the Canadian border, she met and fell in love with the hotel keeper's son, Judd Holland. She and Uncle Judd decided to get married during her Thanksgiving school vacation, and go up to Winnipeg on the train for a brief honeymoon. Again, casting aside conventions, (she's always doing that!) they got the priest out of bed at four-thirty in the morning so they could be married and catch the six o'clock train.

During the Depression, a favorite "Aunt Rosie" story goes, she had a table full of dinner guests and after all had eaten their first helping, she waved a platter over the table asking about seconds for anyone. The platter was empty. Another favorite story, told by those it happened to, was that if you dropped in to visit, she'd say, "How would you like a piece of cake?" If you said yes, she'd scurry to the kitchen and within five minutes she'd have one baking in the oven!

She was part of the Hoy familys' musical tradition. Whenever two or more gathered, she or Aunt Agnes sat at the piano and started a sing-a-long. For over thirty years she played the organ at St. Kevin's Church and for most family weddings, anniversaries and even funerals. For the past five years she has been playing at a nursing home where most of the residents are younger than she.

When Aunt Rosie turned seventy-five she had a routine physical which mystified the doctors. Her carotid arteries were so clogged they wondered how she stayed on her feet. "My four mile hike around Lake Nokomis every day must've helped," she told them. They cleaned out her "pipes" and we hope she's good for another twenty years.

Chapter VIII

Ours was a real Polish wedding—it lasted five days. The mass and bridal breakfast were just the beginning. About sixty guests from out of town spent the rest of the day at our house visiting, enjoying the snacks and spirits, or playing poker in the garage. Some of the more creative women put on a skit. My mother really relied on the good Lord—it could've rained.

After my mother's efficient friends and neighbors put on a buffet supper for about one hundred and fifty people, we all went across the street to the school for our wedding dance. I have been told that people were creeping back to their guest houses with shoes in hand until four o'clock in the morning. Then they stayed in Browerville another day to rest and enjoy the leftovers.

Pete and I left the dance about eleven o'clock to change into our traveling clothes. We had told everyone we were going to Detroit Lakes, about ninety miles north, for our honeymoon so we drove off in that direction. Twenty minutes later we sneaked back into a dear neighbor's house and watched the dance from across the street. They had given us their house as a bridal suite. But we weren't alone. When Pete and I just got settled into bed, we heard a noise.

"What was that?" he asked. Then we heard it again. "UUrrmpphh!" It sounded like the intake of a snore. Peeking into the next room I saw a man lying across the bed, and without thinking, I turned on the light. It was one of our wedding guests—he had stayed too long at the bar. The bright light awakened him and he staggered in and sat on our bed.

"Would you like us to walk you back to the party?" Pete asked, hoping our guest would volunteer to go by himself.

"No, no, no," he shook his head, "I'll be okay right here."

He sat, and sat, and sat. We visited with him the rest of the night. I don't think he remembered it was our wedding night.

At five o'clock in the norning, Pete and I decided we'd be on our way. When we reached Detroit Lakes, I was so tired I drove right into the side of our cabin. I had learned to drive in Washington after Pete and I began dating. It had been traumatic. Each one of his new 1947 Chevrolet fenders had been crumpled in the learning process. I had collided with a Rapid Transit bus, a high curb, and a fire hydrant. Each time he had been tolerant. I thought this would be the last straw. Pete laughed, and in a sing-song voice said, "Confucius say one doesn't get angry with bride on honeymoon." I laughed too, a little nervously.

After a short nap, we heard a knock on our cabin door. "Who is it?" Pete hollered, not too enthusiastically. It was a cousin of mine who lived nearby. "You want to come over for dinner?"

When you come from a large family, privacy is an unknown. Pete was beginning to learn this.

Pete and I delayed our extensive honeymoon trip to California for a month after we were married so that my brother Harry could help me with the driving. None of us had been farther west than the South Dakota border, so it was going to be adventure all the way. It started off with a bang—as I was speeding along the flat, unobstructed highway. "My God! What was that?" Pete yelled.

It sounded as though someone had shot a bullet at our car. We swerved to the ditch. "A blow-out," Harry informed us, gravely shaking his head as he looked at the rear tire. We hadn't gone two hundred miles yet. He and Pete put on the spare, and we had to spend an unplanned twenty dollars for a new tire.

When we reached the hills of South Dakota, it was hot and dusty and I'd already lost my enthusiasm for driving another fifteen hundred miles. I hadn't been "car sick" since I was twelve years old—the time I threw up on my mother's friend's new blanket. But now I was dizzy and my stomach seemed to be rolling with the vibrations of the car. When we drove through rain the windshield wipers went back and forth and my stomach went up and down. The only way I could get over the queasiness was to eat. It was a simple solution until the towns were farther and farther apart. When I felt as though I needed a poached egg on toast RIGHT NOW, and the road sign said "Next gas station, 42 miles", I was desperate. I saw cattle crossing the highway, and I was tempted to kill, just for a piece of meat!

My brother finally said, "You're acting just like a pregnant woman who wants a dill pickle in the middle of the night!" In our naivete that hadn't occurred to us. Pete gasped, "You're pregnant????" The traditional announcement scene had the expectant mother sitting in a rocking chair knitting booties; I was driving a hot car over the flats of Wyoming. It took us two days to digest this new development.

We had borrowed the latest in air conditioners for the car. A long cylinder hung outside the front window. It was filled with water and had a fan in front that revolved with the incoming air. The cool moist air was supposed to keep us comfortable, but it must not have been functioning. The "air conditioning" made the inside temperature and humidity the same—one hundred degrees and one hundred percent.

By the time we reached Arizona, my misery had affected Pete and Harry, but not for long. Pete was enthusiastic about seeing Ernie Pyle's home in Albuquerque; I wanted to lie quietly and die. Finally, we stopped at a motel during the day and then drove through the desert at night. "Looks the same to me," Pete said, as we sped along in the dark. He could always see a little humor in our predicament.

We spent a few days in Los Angeles with some dear relatives, and they devoted several days to showing us around the city. Hollywood and Vine and Beverly Hills were a must. We also saw the twisted and bent remains of the recently burned Hollywood Race Track, Knotts Berry Farm, and some Universal Studio movie sets. I was feeling selfishly miserable.

The drive up the coast was beautiful, but the waves made me seasick. When we arrived in San Francisco more relatives entertained us. The vantage point for seeing the city at night, The Top o' The Mark, was fogged in. As we sat looking out the window at nothing, Pete piped up, "Well, Mary, at least the height won't make you sick."

"So this is what it feels like to be pregnant—ugh!" I thought, as we ended our visit in California. I couldn't stand the smell of cigarettes so I had to quit smoking; I couldn't drink coffee either. Without my two crutches, my caffeine and nicotine, and with a constant wave of nausea, I was a miserable traveling companion—especially to have along on a honeymoon!

We had seen signs "Harold's Club or Bust" wherever we went and had planned to check into it in Reno, but we drove through at night and went right on past. We'd take our chances with the "Bust."

In Yellowstone Park we were lucky to find another cousin working at the Union Pacific Hotel. He was able to get us rooms without reservations. When we ate at the hotel dining room, Pete wanted to treat me to a local specialty—I must try brook trout. When it arrived on a large oval platter, I almost jumped from the chair. It was all there—head, tails, and everything in between. I poked my fork into the body and its eyes popped open. "Take it away!" I gagged and draped it with my napkin. Poor Pete. There was no way to please me. Just take me back to Minnesota.

The next morning we were on hand to watch "Old Faithful" erupt. Every eighty minutes up it went; my stomach was on a similar schedule. Artists' Point, Tower Falls, the cuddly bear cubs were all there for my pleasure. All I wanted was to quit moving.

Chapter IX

It was not you who chose me,
It was I who commissioned you
To go forth and bear fruit.
Your fruit must endure,
So that all you ask the Father in my name
He will give you.

John 15:16 (Old Confraternity).

In late August, 1949, Pete and I went back to Washington to get settled before he had to go to school. We found an upstairs apartment near the zoo on Irving Street Northwest. It was on the bus line to Catholic University, so Pete could travel alone. He counted eighty-two steps from the front of our house to the corner—and he very rarely missed our sidewalk.

I was no longer nauseated and started to feel like I wanted to live. Years later I read in *Life* magazine how I should have felt all along.

Whatever feelings pregnancy may arouse—delight, indifference, resignation or horror—the very idea of creating a new human being is awesome. Pregnancy is surely the most creative thing you will ever do—even if you have done it inadvertently. And the process itself is miraculous—so hard to believe that at an already appointed hour you will divide like some ancient cell, and suddenly it won't just be you any longer but you and some other being, to whom you will be tied, by nerves, and tissue and chemistry, all your life. This being is already within you, shouting in a sometimes deafening voice, look out, stand back, here comes a whole new person. And you are the lifeline, its substance, its nourishment. Only you can make sure that its bones are strong and its eyes are clear. How good you must be, how well behaved, how faithful to this being.*

Pete was excited about becoming a father. His only brother was two years younger than he so he had no experience with babies. One night I found him cuddling his big old shoe in his arms. "What in heaven's name are you doing?" I asked.

"Practicing," he said as he patted the sole, "I've never held a new baby before."

I thought I was a pro. I was fourteen when my youngest brother was born prematurely at home. He weighed under four pounds, was less than a foot long, and snuggled comfortably in a cigar box. If I could take care of him, I certainly was ready to be a mother. I had worked in the pediatric and maternity wards—I knew everything about having babies. When Dr. Hawken, my obstetrician, announced in November that any day I should begin to feel life, I very innocently asked, "Should I call and let you know?" I had a lot to learn.

Each time I went to his office on 16th and M Street I stopped across the street at St. Matthews Cathedral to pay a visit. I always knelt at a beautiful statue of the Blessed Virgin; I was fascinated by the warmth of her eyes. She was a mother and I could tell her how scared I was.

During our first Christmas together we started a Christmas Eve tradition that has lasted through twenty-eight years. I read the story of the Birth of Jesus from the Gospel of St. Luke and Pete put the infant in the crib. Then we drank a glass of wine and sang "Happy Birthday to Jesus" and "Silent Night." After our ceremony Santa Claus came and we enjoyed the commercial part of Christmas.

About the middle of February I began to set up a nursery for

* Excerpt from "A Woman on Her Way to a Miracle," by Eleanor Graves. LIFE Magazine, (c) 1966 Time, Inc. Reprinted with permission.

our baby—I bought a second-hand wardrobe chest, refinished it, and decorated it with pink and blue decals. I wandered through the infants' department at Woodward and Lothrop's and self-consciously picked out the basic layette—diapers, shirts, kimonos, and blankets. It was like playing house, only I was twenty-seven years old.

Every afternoon when Pete came home from school his first question was, "Will this be the night?" I was getting big and uncomfortable; when you're an even five feet, the baby takes up most of your middle. I had difficulty fitting under the steering wheel and reaching the clutch, so we stayed close to home.

On Saturday, March 11, we had asked my brother Harry and Pete's Aunt Alice to come for dinner. All afternoon I dragged myself around the kitchen feeling something different was happening to me. Were these contractions? I put the dinner on without mentioning my anxiety to Pete, but after we had eaten I whispered, "I think I'm in labor—ask Harry to take Aunt Alice home NOW!"

A novice at being a new father, Pete wanted to go right to the hospital, but I wanted to wait. Dr. Hawken had said to call him when the contractions were fifteen minutes apart, and about midnight they were. I stalled until two o'clock, when my membranes ruptured. Then we both panicked. I grabbed some towels and Pete grabbed the suitcase I'd packed a month before, and we went out into the night, surprised at how quiet it was. It was raining. I don't know whom we expected to be there as we walked out onto Irving Street; at that hour even the zoo was quiet.

Pete held my arm and we started up toward 14th Street. "Don't worry, Mary, we'll find a cab," he reassured me. He sounded just like St. Joseph! God must take care of first time parents. In the next block a noisy party of people was getting out of a taxi. Pete whistled and waved and stepped out into the street. I was amazed and relieved when I saw the light on the top of the cab coming our way. By this time my towels were drenched with rain and amniotic fluid!

At the hospital the girl at the admitting desk took all the pertinent information and then turned to Pete. "You can go back home now, sir. We'll call you when your wife delivers."

"W-w-wh-a-a-tt?" Pete stammered.

"That's our hospital policy, sir. Would you like to have me call you a cab?" He couldn't fight an institution like Columbia Hospital for Women. It had opened its doors on March 4, 1866, because of the large number of females who came to Washington during the Civil War, and more than 100,000 babies had been born there before our arrival.

So off he went, and up I went. What was supposed to be the happiest time of our life was the most desolate for both of us, but it didn't last long. Two hours later, at four forty-three, our baby boy was born. Dr. Hawken called Pete, and Pete called both sets of grandparents, although it was only four o'clock in Minnesota. This was the first grandchild for both families so there was much rejoicing. Then Pete announced the arrival of this new seven pound miracle to everyone who would listen that early in the morning.

We named him James Joseph after my brother and Pete's brother. We had launched our planned parenthood.

When the *Washington Post* interviewed Pete before our wedding, he told them I wanted six children. I've been regretting those words ever since.

"You didn't want me!" complains number seven.

"How come you had me?" asks number nine.

"You shoulda quit at six!" number six sulks.

Chapter X

When Jim was three months old and Pete was out of school for the summer, we took our first trip as a family. It would have been easier if I had been breast-feeding Jim, but after a month of trying, he wasn't gaining weight, so the pediatrician suggested switching to Similac. We packed bottles, formula, bottle warmer, his own spoon and dish, baby food, car bed, bassinette, crib sheets, diaper pail. You would have thought we were going to the Sahara sand dunes where nothing was available, instead of to Minnesota. A priest friend offered to help with the driving for a free ride home. He paid dearly. When he wasn't driving, he was feeding or changing Jim. We had stocked our car with the first attempt at disposable diapers and before ecology was a household word, disposable meant you tossed them out the car window. We left a trail of these soiled remnants along the highway for twelve hundred miles.

Pete and I celebrated our first wedding anniversary during this trip to Minnesota. As we were on our way to dinner, I announced very timorously, "Guess what, Pete? We're going to have another baby."

"What? You don't mean—you can't—gosh! Are you sure? When?"

"In February, as near as I can figure."

"Well!" Pete breathed a heavy sigh. "What d'ya know! That's kind of soon, isn't it? Jim will be eleven months—."

"Harry and I are only eleven months apart. We thought it was

43

nice being that close. In fact, for about six weeks every year we were the same age and we told people we were twins. Then, on December 17, I'd gain a year on him. I don't know how my mother liked it though."

"Mary, are you feeling O.K.? I hope you won't be as miserable as you were the last time."

"I don't like to remember the last time. I just quit smoking again, had you noticed? That's all that's bothered me so far."

"Mmmm, wouldn't it be nice to have a little girl?"

In our second winter of marriage, we bought our first home. We wanted to be closer to Catholic University, but apartments nearby were scarce. With loans from both of our parents, we made the down payment and became "home owners"—the dream of every young couple after World War II.

My second pregnancy was easier. I accepted the first three months of nausea as part of the package and appreciated the good health I enjoyed the remaining six months. Dr. Hawken remembered our middle-of-the-night taxi ride to the hospital when Jim was born. The first week of February he announced, "Well, you're due next week, Mary. If you don't go into labor by the eighth, come in to the hospital and we'll start things going." That winter we had a Catholic University student, Roy Montgomery, living with us. Instead of paying for his room and board, he took notes and read for Pete, helped take care of Jim, and did some chauffering. On February 8, Pete, Jim, and Roy took me to the hospital; but once again, according to hospital policy, they left me at the door. I had to go in alone. That night Dr. Hawken began the induction, and by noon the next day we had a beautiful daughter, Elizabeth Ann. My great grandmother was Elizabeth Duffy, my mother was Elizabeth Hoy, and I was Mary Elizabeth. It was a strong name, meaning "consecrated to God."

Our friends congratulated us, "A boy and a girl, that's a nice family." We thought so, too. Jim was eleven months old, still on the bottle and still in diapers, so Pete had to help me with the nursery routine. When it was time for the two o'clock feeding each morning, he warmed the bottle while I changed the diaper. The "how to" books on baby care were still preaching "sterile technique" with the formula, so Pete was careful when he flipped

the nipple. He also learned how to flush out the soiled diapers in
the toilet and to wash them in a wringer washing machine. On
weekends, he enjoyed hanging out the "daily dozen" on the
clothesline—for us it was two dozen.

On our second anniversary, I said, "Guess what, Pete?"

"Don't tell me", he said. "Let me guess. You're pregnant
again." All Pete did was shake his head. It seemed that God was
commissioning us too fast. We hadn't planned to populate the
world by ourselves.

In July of 1951, two years after we were married, Pete and I
drove up to Boston to the Blinded Veterans Convention. He took
me to his old summer cottage near Lowell. The blinded veterans
took a boat ride to Provincetown on the tip of Cape Cod and
although the noise of the motor drowned them out, they held
their meeting enroute. Pete was elected National President and
according to him, "I was the loudest candidate." We had left the
two children with Pete's mother and father, and they were as glad
to see us as we were to be back.

It was Pete's senior year at school, but he didn't have the time
or money to enjoy the social life and camaraderie that other college students had. I remember only one night that he went out for
a "beer with the boys." He was back by ten o'clock. He did all
his studying with readers in an office on campus; when he came
home he was husband, daddy, dishwasher, baby sitter, and general handyman.

Our social life revolved around our family. We had given huge
christening parties for Jim and Elizabeth, we celebrated each
person's birthday including grandparents, aunts, uncles, and
great-aunts. The holidays became traditional family celebrations,
and Christmas especially took on a new meaning with young
children in the house. Jim could put the infant in the crib.
Elizabeth could hang an ornament on the tree with a little help
from her daddy. With two sets of grandparents showering them
with gifts, our hearts and toy box were full. With Christmas money
I went to the January sales at Garfinkels and bought winter coat
and cap sets for Jim and Elizabeth for half their original price.
These outfits were handed down for ten years!

But we had to plan for our next baby. On the 18th of February, a dear friend, Miriam, who was almost five months pregnant, went with me to the commissary in southwest Washington. Disabled veterans could buy groceries there, and I wanted to stock our larder for the next few weeks when I'd be housebound. Miriam and I drove over the cobblestone streets enjoying the historical sights and the bumpy ride. It was like a step back a hundred years into early Washington. Later in the afternoon after we had returned home, I began to feel abdominal pressure with slight contractions. Pete was still at school so I called Miriam. "Miriam, I think I'm in labor!"

She laughed hysterically. I didn't think it was so funny. "It's unreal!" she exclaimed.

"What's unreal? I'm due any day now."

"Either our timing is coordinated or the cobblestone streets got to both of us."

"You don't mean you—"

"Mary, I felt life for the first time after we got home."

"Oh, thank God." I said, much relieved. I knew she wasn't due yet.

"I feel just like St. Elizabeth. The babe in *my* womb leaped!"

After midnight, with a seminary friend from across the street, Pete and I made one more trip to the Columbia Hospital for Women. And once more he was sent home to wait—but again, not for long. At five-thirty in the morning the phone rang and Pete was awake to answer it.

"Mr. McKenna, this is Dr. Hawken. Congratulations on your new baby daughter. She is especially fortunate; she was born with the caul."

"With the what?" Pete stammered. He knew of people called to the convent or called home to Heaven. He wasn't ready for his daughter to go either place. "With the c-a-u-l," Dr. Hawken spelled out. "The amniotic sac was fully intact so her head is shaped perfectly. The old New England fishermen thought this was a good omen. They would dry the sac and put it on the masthead of their fishing boat for good luck. She'll be a child of fortune! Your wife is fine, too. You can come to the hospital now if you wish."

"At this hour?" Pete thought. He called his folks and they

came right over. His Aunt Nellie came along to stay with Jim and Elizabeth.

Jim was twenty-three months old and still in diapers part of the time. Elizabeth was a year old, still on the bottle and in diapers. With a new baby we had a relay of schedules. Pete asked one day as he was putting the thirtieth diaper through the wringer, "Why didn't we do it up right? It probably would've been easier to have triplets!"

I loved babies and was in my glory when I could feel the warmth and joy of cuddling them. New babies were never much care, but I tried to spend their feeding time exclusively with them. Their gurgling and their smiles made me their slave. I enjoyed rocking all three of the babies and singing their favorite lullabyes.

Early in May as I skimmed through the morning mail I sorted the bills, the junk mail, the Mother's Day cards, and then I saw the return address on the next envelope: THE WHITE HOUSE. "The White House?" I shouted to myself. "Who do we know at the White House?" My first instinct was to rip it open, but instead I just looked at it, checked to be sure it was addressed to us, and then slowly and neatly cut the edge open with the scissors. I felt as though I were handling a historic document.

> *President and Mrs. Harry S. Truman*
> *request the honour of your presence*
> *at the White House Garden Party*
> *to honour the disabled veterans of our country*
> *on Thursday, the fifth day of June*
> *Nineteen hundred and fifty-two*
> *from two-thirty until four o'clock.*

"The White House! Mommy and Daddy are going to the White House!" I shouted as I picked up Jim and danced around the living room. He was just learning colors and he couldn't get too excited about a white house. Most houses in Washington were red brick! He couldn't understand my sudden burst of exuberance.

I wished Pete were home to share this moment, but it would have to keep until he came home from school at five.

When I told him the exciting news, he just smiled. "Must be

one of the fringe benefits of being president of the BVA. You stick with me, Kid, and you'll get right to the top!'' Maybe it was a good thing I had my rapturous moment without him when the mail came that morning.

When June 5 finally came, four days before Pete's graduation, we had already enjoyed the anticipation with our family and friends. It was a day to remember. When we arrived at the White House gate, we were ushered to the ''garden'' and as Pete and I stood under a trellis of roses, I nudged him. ''There's a poor old blind man standing alone; should we see if we can help him?''

''Sir, we are Pete and Mary McKenna from the Blinded Veterans Association. Would you care to join us and walk over to listen to the music?''

''Hi, I'm Mel Maas. Sure nice of you to offer. I haven't been blind very long and I'm just beginning to learn my way around,'' he said as he grabbed my other arm.

The reception was held on the west lawn because the White House had been gutted for renovations. As the three of us stood listening to the Marine Band, a military man, heavy with medals, and his wife came up and shook our new friend's hand. Then he introduced Mel to his wife. ''Helen, this is General Melvin Maas. The Major General and I were at Quantico Marine Base together.''

I nudged Pete again and whispered, ''What you do for the LEAST of my brethren!''

Margaret Truman was the official hostess, as Bess stood on the steps and watched. We were sitting on folding chairs near the band and as I saw her coming, I announced, ''Pete, Margaret Truman is coming with our punch.''

He jumped to his feet in proper Boston style and knocked the glass from her hand.

''I'm so sorry,'' she said as she tried to retrieve the falling glass. ''I hope I didn't spill any on you.''

''I'm sorry, too,'' Pete apologized, ''but my mother taught me to always stand up for a lady.''

Margaret handed him another glass, then quickly took it back. ''Oops! This will never do.'' As she emptied it on the ground I saw a fly in it. She gave him a third glass. "Let's try one more time," she said with a big Margaret Truman smile.

"Miss Truman," I said somewhat timidly, "we had a baby girl in February and we named her Margaret. Would you like to see her picture?" Pete was cringing. "You had to be from the midwest to say something like that," he told me later.

"I'd love to," she said graciously. "In fact, let me use your pen and I'll sign it for her."

Our daughter has always treasured her baby picture with "Best wishes to Margaret, from Margaret Truman."

We shook hands with President Truman, who winced behind his thick glasses as he saw Pete's face. We met J. Lawton Collins, Anna Rosenburg, Charles Brennan, and other cabinet members. I wanted to shout "Daughter of Browerville, you've come a long way!"

Chapter XI

On June 9, 1952, our third wedding anniversary, Pete graduated from Catholic University. His mother and I cried tears of joy when he went up to get his diploma. Our cup runneth over. We had three healthy children and "everything we asked in His name." Pete decided he wanted to study for his master's degree at the University of Minnesota.

"Do you remember how cold it was, when we flew up there before we were married?" I asked.

"Sure do. I loved it," he said cockily, perhaps remembering the eye-opener my mother gave him each morning. "It couldn't be any worse than the heat here in the summer. Besides I was stationed in Wisconsin and Upper Michigan during the war."

Selling our house and moving our family to Minnesota seemed like a huge project. The first hurdle was easy. Pete's folks decided to assume our mortgage and buy the house. Both his mother and father worked in northeast Washington so it would be handy to work and less driving for them. Another piece of good fortune for us was my brother James' wedding at the Notre Dame chapel in South Bend, Indiana, on May 31, 1952. We took Jim and Elizabeth with us and met my folks there. They took the two grandchildren back to Minnesota with them. All we had left to do was get Pete graduated, pack our household possessions, hire a mover and drive the car with Pete and baby Margaret to Minneapolis, twelve hundred miles away.

We arrived on Flag Day, June 14, and Pete thought it appropriate that all the flags should fly on the day he adopted Minnesota as
his home. Our gala reception was short-lived when we reached
my Aunt Florence's house. We had left the key and a check for
four hundred and fifty dollars with her and we thought our furniture would be unloaded at 1087 Fifteenth Avenue Southeast when
we arrived. Instead the moving van was parked at her door.
"Sorry, lady," the truck driver explained, "our instructions are
to pick up the key and payment in cash. I can't take your check.
Sorry."

"In cash?" I asked unbelievingly. I had a lot to learn about
moving. "We don't have even one hundred in cash. Where can
we cash a check? It's four-thirty—I'm sure the banks are
closed."

When Aunt Florence heard our predicament, that we didn't
have the money, she thought fast, "I have a friend who has a bill
paying service. She'll cash a check for you if I call her." And she
did. After three days of driving God knew we didn't need any
more problems. He always came through with an answer.

We were hardly settled when we had to plan another trip. As
President of the Blinded Veterans, Pete had to attend the convention in San Francisco in July of '52. My brother, Father Dick,
offered to help me drive. I had bad memories of our last trip to
California, but this time I wasn't pregnant, I thought. We had a
suite of rooms at the Palace hotel, and we were expected to be
host and hostess at the convention. After being the honored guests
at a luncheon as the "first lady", I went back to our room to rest.
Suddenly, I felt stomach cramps and waves of nausea. I lost my
lunch and after an hour of retching, the hotel doctor came up and
examined me. "What did you eat?" he asked.

"Chicken a la king," I told him, almost losing it again.

"They've had trouble with that before," he acknowledged.
"You probably have food poisoning."

During the parade, instead of riding in a prominent car, I was
barely hanging my head out the window on the fourteenth floor to
get a glimpse of it. I languished in our room amid flowers and
get-well messages—I remembered the same queasy feeling before.
We didn't tell the other conventioneers that we suspected another

pregnancy, but later that year when the BVA chaplain, Father
Carroll, was going through Minneapolis, he called me. "Did you
get over the food poisoning?" he asked.

"No, Father, it seems it was a chronic condition. It usually
lasts nine months."

The return trip was as miserable as that unforgettable honeymoon.

Pete loved Minnesota and especially the University. He had
good memories of the Big Ten football teams of the thirties. They
weren't so great anymore, and anyway we couldn't afford to buy
tickets and hire a baby sitter to go. We did watch the bonfires and
fraternity house decorations at homecoming. Throughout all our
baby rearing years we indulged in two luxuries—we didn't spend
very much on fancy food or clothing and we didn't buy liquor or
go out to eat very often, but I had a cleaning woman each week
and we always budgeted for trips in the summer. We decided
what was important for us. When the cleaning lady came, she also
took care of the children while I kept my routine appointments
with my obstetrician. We got our ten dollars worth!

Our first Christmas in Minnesota was memorable. Pete's folks
came from Washington and mine from Browerville. Several of my
brothers and my sister plus aunts and uncles were all with us.
After the Nativity scene tradition we exchanged our gifts and all
the adults found a toy to play with.

By this time my mother had established what became her annual routine—she made pajamas or nighties for each grandchild.
They wore them on Christmas Eve. She kept this up until she was
making over twenty garments—then cataracts and a detached ret-
ina made it difficult for her to sew.

God always had great things happening to us whenever we
needed help. Early in 1953 my sister Jackie came to live with us.
She worked nearby at the University Hospital as a scrub nurse in
eye surgery. We had some gory stories at our dinner table. "We
did an evisceration today. The doctor laid the eyeball—"

"Ugh! Not while we eat—"

She was a big help with the babies, and they loved her.

On April 19, early on a Sunday morning, I started to go into
labor. I awakened Pete, and we decided I should drive over to St.

Mary's Hospital and have my sister stay with the three children. I walked quietly into their bedroom and breathed a quiet goodbye. They looked so angelic in their sleep that I didn't want to leave them. However, my time had come. Pete and I sat outside in the car until the contractions were coming every five minutes. We didn't know that he could have come in with me—right to the labor room. Our new obstetrician, Dr. McCaffrey, wasn't familiar with my modus operandi, so I told the labor room nurse to send me right into delivery. She did, and I delivered a six pound, twelve ounce baby boy within thirty minutes. Afterward Dr. McCaffrey took Pete to the chapel for mass and then drove him to our house. What a contrast to the cool, detached treatment he got in Washington. We named our son John David. "John" was my maiden name—it seemed a strong name and a fourth child would need it. Once again we heard, "Two boys and two girls—now that's a nice family."

In the summer of 1953 the Blinded Veterans Convention was held in Philadelphia. Since our way had been paid to the one in San Francisco the previous year, we felt we should make an effort to attend this one. My brother Father Dick and my sister Jackie came along so the driving was easy. We were fortunate that my parents and cousins were willing to take care of our younger children while we traveled with the older ones. The grandparents in Washington were always happy to see them, too.

Whenever and wherever we've driven on the east coast we've always included visits to relatives and friends along the way. I've taken much ribbing about dropping in on people (always with forewarning, though) as much as two hundred miles out of our way. Pete calls me a "looker upper." I've discovered relatives of Pete's that he never knew existed, both alive and in cemeteries. He has just enough New England in him to be reserved about things like that. I had written to some of his relatives for years before I met them. Years later, in Valley Falls, Rhode Island, we found his grandparents' gravestone underneath the sod. We cleaned it off and set it upright with our hope that it would remain for posterity.

I knew about my ancestors. My great-grandparents had come from Ireland and Poland in the middle 1800's and had established homes and families that gave a sense of continuity to my life. I can visit their graves, see the farms they cleared and settled, and feel a touch of the past become a part of the here and now. I remember my grandparents, and I feel that their hard work and philosophy of life was passed on to my parents, then to me, to my children and even to my grandchildren. I hoped we could learn more about the other half of our children's forebears.

Chapter XII

Pete's second year at the University was interesting. It was the Year of the "MMPI." He chose as his thesis the question of whether it made a difference in the test scores if the Minnesota Multiphasic Personality Inventory were given by a written or oral test. The purpose was to establish if it was a fair test for blind people. He picked as his subjects one hundred University students from six hundred random post office box numbers. Each student took the oral test and then two weeks later the written. Pete and his readers compared the profiles from both, and came to the conclusion that there was no significant difference.

It was a proud night for us on March 18, 1954, when he received his Master of Arts degree in vocational guidance and counseling. His mother flew in from Washington, and we had a big party in Pete's honor. After seven years of Braille notes, Audiograph recordings, and learning his way around two college campuses, he had attained the first part of his goal: a job in his field was next.

We started at the top in February by writing to the Office of Vocational Rehabilitation in the Department of Health, Education and Welfare in Washington, D.C. "Thank you for your letter of February 7 in which you express an interest in doing guidance work with the visually handicapped," they wrote back. "We do not have any positions on our staff where your particular qualifications can be utilized. A position such as this is usually found in the State agency which is responsible for providing services to disabled individuals. . . ."

Then we wrote to the State Vocational Rehabilitation Centers
and Divisions for the Blind in all the states we'd like to live in,
beginning with our own. We wrote to twenty-three states, and
only two of them gave any hope of a job—"sometime in the
future." They were all polite and wished him well. The Chicago
Regional Office of Vocational Rehabilitation wrote, "Frankly
speaking, there are no positions open in which you might be interested. In fact, the present national situation is one of retrench-
ment rather than of employment of new workers."

We wrote to the schools for the blind—no vacancies. The Minneapolis Public School System was not ready to try a blind
teacher. "It's never been done," they explained.

Recently I saw the television story of David Ticchi, a young
seventh grade English teacher in Newton, Massachusetts. He had
been turned down by four or five schools because he was blind.
His colleagues assessed his teaching as "impressive"—the
youngsters take responsibility for order, they talk about his being
different without embarrassment, there is a minimum of noise,
and with the help of volunteers for grading papers, he is able to
function successfully in the classroom. In 1974 there were two
hundred and seventy-two blind teachers in schools in the United
States. We've come a long way.

The Office of Education in HEW wrote, "I regret not being able
to give you more specific help. Meanwhile, let me wish you every
success in your chosen field."

A letter from an employment agency to the Ford Foundation
stated: "I have had your organization recommended to me as
being a likely organization to turn to in regards to a man that we
have been sincerely trying to help. I am contacting you as I have
exhausted every possible facility that I can think of, in this area,
to find employment for him. As you will notice I have been working on this man since March 22, or better than a month, and have
been unable to find a company or an organization that feels able
to utilize his services.

"I would like to state that this man called on me at my office
without the assistance of a dog or any person to show him around,
and in a matter of a few minutes, I found him to be very persona-

ble and very capable. As a matter of fact in the first five minutes I almost forgot that he was totally blind.

"It is my belief that this man's education and abilities could be very well utilized in industry in a personnel counseling capacity. I am wondering if you would give him your most sincere consideration and advise this office as to what possibilities you may have for him."

The New York State Commission for the Blind wrote, "I am sorry that our reply must be so discouraging, but it is the best we can do. We feel that you would wish an honest statement rather than an evasive one."

About ninety-nine percent of our replies said, "We'll keep your name on file."

But in 1954 each day there was a new defeat. Finally, there was an opening in the Vocational Rehabilitation Department in St. Paul. Pete went right over to apply. He came home dejected. "What did they say?" I asked sympathetically.

" 'Sorry, Mr. McKenna, we just don't think you could handle the travel and testing that would be involved in this job.' How do they know I can't?"

"Didn't you tell them about all your work on your thesis with the MMPI?"

"They just decided that a blind man can't handle it, and that's that. Was there any mail today?"

"Oh, yah, a real nice letter from Father Carroll. He's got a new twist for you to consider. I'll read it to you." Father Carroll had been the chaplain at the Avon Rehab Center and also visited Pete at Valley Forge Hospital. We looked forward to seeing him at the Blinded Veterans Conventions whenever we went. He was their chaplain, too.

"Dear Pete: I don't know when this letter will finally get typed, but as I am dictating it on the 15th of March, it should reach you not too long after your graduation.

"Congratulations on the Master's Degree, and all best wishes for successful placement. I am writing to the Foundation for you as you suggested.

"Now for a few words with regard to your future: I hope that you will do everything in your power to stay out of work with the blind for a period of at least five years, preferably ten.

"The reason for stating this is your request that I send in references to the American Foundation. Basically my reason is that I feel if you ever want to come into this work, you will give to it tremendously more value if you come to it from outside, from other areas of interest.

"I know you have the practical question of feeding all the little mouths, but I also know there is a question of emphasis in where you seek work. So for what my experience and background are worth, take this as considered advice, put your emphasis entirely on work among sighted people and not in an organization for the blind. God be with you. Sincerely yours in Christ, Thomas J. Carroll."

Pete never got as depressed as I. "Do you realize," he'd say, "that as long as I'm not working, you have the best educated laundry man in the block?" We still had three in diapers.

Meanwhile back in the nursery—nine months after the BVA Convention in the City of Brotherly Love, on May 6, Mary Catherine joined our family. She was especially dear because she was a breach birth (born feet first with the cord around her neck). The other children were thrilled to have a new baby sister. Some of our friends suggested we either quit going to conventions, or maybe we'd like to try the rhythm method. Even the Church was pushing it. Cana Club speakers all over the country were drawing temperature charts and trying to explain this "approved" method of birth control! We hadn't even been married five years, and she was our fifth child—maybe we were rushing things.

Chapter XIII

Each time we had a new baby, I bought a new baby book, and I tried to get the same kind, *A Catholic Baby's Record,* because it was easy to keep up. I didn't have a lot of time to record their weight every month, or when each tooth came in, but this one had the important personal events in each child's life. Shortly after Mary Catherine was born, I went to downtown Minneapolis to buy my annual book. After parking in a lot and walking two blocks, I found the Catholic Gift Shop was out of *A Catholic Baby's Record.* They had others, but I wanted this particular one. I called several religious goods stores and located my book on the other side of St. Paul. Did everyone have this much trouble finding religious gifts? In my frustration, wheels started turning in my head—Pete is always dubious when I say, "You know, I've been thinking" or "I have an idea."

In 1954 there were no suburban shopping areas, and I thought there was a need for a religious gift shop away from downtown. I asked Pete if he'd like to go to dinner at the Criterion Restaurant—it was always easier to push a plan over cocktails and candlelight rather than in our kitchen full of hungry babies. "But we don't know anything about running a business," he protested.

"You took a course in small business when you were rehabilitated at Avon. And this certainly will be small. Besides, I used to work in Dad's general store. We both know all about Catholic religious articles."

We prayed. We plotted. We looked for a suitable place to open a shop. Whenever we needed direction, the Holy Spirit was present to give it. We found a house in a commercial zone in Richfield, the first suburb south of Minneapolis. Lyndale Avenue was one of the main streets, so we'd have exposure to heavy traffic. With loans from our families and carpenter work from Pete's mother and dad, we finished the upstairs into bedrooms and turned the living room into a gift shop. It took all summer to re-design the house, find store fixtures, and advertise our new venture. With more loans from relatives, we bought a thousand dollars worth of stock. Our advisor was Father Benno Mischke who was the buyer for the Crosier Fathers. Even in 1954, a thousand dollars didn't buy much, but we spread out the statues, rosaries, medals and chains, and books so that the shelves and counters looked covered.

"What are we going to call our shop?" the new proprietor asked. "We can't use 'The Catholic Gift Shop'—even though that's what it is." We tossed around several possibilities such as "Pete's Place", "The Book & Bible Shop", or "Catholic Supplies." When we realized we would be in Assumption Parish which was emphasizing the Marian Year (one hundred years since the dogma of the Immaculate Conception was established) Pete came up with a name. "We need all the help we can get. Why not call it 'The Marian Shop' and dedicate it to the Mother of God?"

"Great idea, Pete. We'll have our grand opening on August 15, the Feast of the Assumption. It's got to be a success!"

It wasn't instant, but it was a success. The churches in the area gave us publicity and let us sell religious articles at their dinners, fairs and missions. In the mid-fifties the baby boom babies were starting school, making their First Communion and being confirmed. In our business this meant selling prayer books, medals and chains, rosaries, veils, and greeting cards. Our Christmas business swamped us. I had to drive to the wholesale house and reorder the stock as fast as Pete sold it. We were both learning a lot, enjoying the contact with people, and breaking even financially.

With five young children and our growing business, we thought we had our hands full. We decided we had better try the rhythm routine, so I slept with a thermometer taped to the head of our bed. Every morning, ignoring the baby's crying and toddlers' demands, I took my temperature and recorded it on the graph. Then one morning it happened; I put the thermometer under my tongue and got nauseated. I was pregnant again!

The summer of 1955 was long and hot. I had never gone through the summer "heavy with child" before—our babies were all born from February to May. When my delivery time came, the second week of October, I arranged to send the pre-school children to my cousin's house. The house was clean and quiet, the groceries were in, the laundry done.

"I can't waste this precious baby-sitting time," I told myself. I took an ounce of castor oil. About eleven o'clock that night my contractions started. I called a cousin's husband who had promised to drive me to the hospital, "Jerry, come quick. Maybe you should get a police escort." He was there in five minutes and twenty minutes later I was wheeled into the elevator and up to the delivery room. Before the nun anesthetist could get her coif on, the delivery room nurse called and told her not to bother. Our son Joseph Francis had arrived.

People were still adding up the sexes. "Three boys and three girls, now that's enough family." Anyone who has more than four children knows that after that it doesn't make any difference. You can't buy a half dozen of anything any more, you can't live in a three bedroom house, and you never get invited to anyone's house for dinner. You are a Large Family.

Chapter XIV

Happy are you who fear the Lord,
who walk in his ways!
For you shall eat the fruit of
your handiwork;
happy shall you be, and favored.
Your wife shall be like a fruitful vine
in the recesses of your home;
Your children like olive plants
around your table.

Psalm 128.

We were happy; we were blessed. We had six children, the eldest just five and a half years old. Our business had increased so much that we outgrew our living-room-turned-shop. Our family had outgrown the tiny quarters in the back and needed the living room space. We bought ten feet of land from our neighbor at $33.97 per month for three years, and began construction of a shop attached to our house. It was exciting for our children to watch the bulldozer dig out the basement, the carpenters frame in the large room and office, and finally break through our bedroom with a door to "the shop." We had another grand opening—this time to thank all our customers.

Pete had his Talking Book, a record player loaned to him by State Services for the Blind, in the office so he could read when he wasn't waiting on customers. For many years Pete had been enjoying this service from the Library Of Congress. He'd get a catalog of available books, send in his order, and the mailman would deliver one or two books each week. The entire service is free to blind people.

A cousin put a bell on the door so Pete could hear when anyone came in. We also had a buzzer he could push if he wanted me from the kitchen. I'd pick up the phone and he'd ask, "Where are the extra five-dollar St. Joseph missals? Can we order a statue of St. Camillus? Will you tell this lady why her rosary turned green?"

It got a little hectic behind the scenes when I had to leave a baby half-changed, meat half-cooked, or wash the garden dirt off to go in and do a deluxe gift wrapping job.

It wasn't all work though. We picnicked every weekend. A telephone call would have a dozen aunts, uncles, and cousins assembled at Minnehaha Park within an hour for a full meal or just doughnuts, coffee, and Kool-aid. Every Sunday evening our family gathered with hot chocolate and sandwiches to watch "Lassie." I had read the story to them before it became serialized.

We had birthday parties once or twice a month from February to May. Sometimes we went all out for these parties—a sleigh ride, skating party, or inviting lots of kids, sometimes just the family. Each child's birthday was a big event. When John, whose birthday usually came in Holy Week, was six we planned a party with his friends, but when he awoke on the 19th of April his face, neck, and chest were peppered with measles. We had to call off the party. "Do big people get measles?" John asked.

"No, not usually," I said.

"Then ask Dr. and Mrs. Erickson to come over. They'll be safe." They came over from their house next door, put on the birthday hats and had just as much fun as any six-year-olds. We sang a very discordant "Happy Birthday" song that is still a treat, even long distance, to our sons away from home.

We tried to keep close to the grandparents in Washington, D.C., by driving there every year or two. Other years they came to visit us. Even a trip to my parents in Browerville, one hundred and forty miles away, made the launching of the *Queen Mary* look like a snap. We had to lay out sixteen outfits, one to wear and one for spare for each of us. The box of "necessities" had dwindled greatly since our first trip with Jim. We had an "amusement box" with colors, books, puzzles, and baby toys, a wet wash cloth, and an emergency bucket.

We used every free opportunity to enrich our children's lives. When President Eisenhower came to Minnesota during his campaign for re-election, we all stood at the ropes to see his plane land. Jim, Elizabeth, Margaret and John had been to his home, the White House, in Washington. Every summer we went to Como Zoo to sit on the turtle, see the baboons and monkeys, and as a special treat, ring the bell on the steam engine. It was many years later, when they went by themselves, that they discovered the other features of Como Park—the rides and carnival. When United Airlines had an open house, we took all the children, most of whom had never flown, through the airplane.

On Halloween (Eve of All Saints) each child dressed up as a saint and marched in the procession at church. We had Saints Piux X, Elizabeth of Hungary, Margaret Mary, Joseph the Worker, and even St. Anthony and Child (Peter III). They learned about the saints they portrayed.

In 1958 we joined two hundred and twenty-four thousand people at Father Peyton's Rosary Rally on the Capitol steps in St. Paul. Every May Day we marched in the Minneapolis parade to honor the Mother of God. Along with most Catholic families, we pledged to say the rosary every day and kept our promise for almost ten years.

About the middle of 1957 we discovered I was pregnant again. It had been almost two years since Joe was born and we were quite satisfied with our half dozen. They were all healthy and happy and we were managing just fine. After the usual nausea of the first three months, I was excited again about another baby. Pete and I decided that if God gave us the six children we wanted, we'd also accept any bonuses He had in mind for us.

The business became a family affair. As soon as a child could see over the counter and count out change, he was taught to wait on customers. Every spring and fall our advertising crew (every child who could walk) put hand bills on the cars at neighboring churches. We formed a chain gang to unload merchandise and put it in our basement warehouse.

It was difficult working through our Christmas rush that year, but the older children were helpful in the shop and the house. I could barely fit behind the wheel to go to the wholesale house for more stock.

The first Sunday after New Year's in 1958 Pete took Jim, Elizabeth and Margaret to the skating rink at nearby Wood Lake. John, Mary Catherine and Joe stayed home for their naps. As I lay on the davenport trying to fit my bulging tummy comfortably on one side, then another, I suddenly felt an oozing. I brought up my hand covered with blood. I tried to get up. Then I began to hemorrhage.

"John David", I called, hoping my four-year-old wouldn't be asleep. He came in bleary-eyed, pretending he'd been sleeping.

I had to stay calm. "Honey, will you take the phone off the hook and dial a number for me?" He dialed slowly UN 9-7330. Our babysitter lived near the skating rink and she ran over to get Pete. Twenty minutes later he rushed in breathless and called the doctor at once.

"But get him at his country club!" I heard him telling the answering service.

Within forty minutes Dr. McCaffrey was at our house. He ordered an ambulance, the baby sitter came, and we were off to St. Mary's. After an hour of examining, taking fetal heartbeats and X-rays, they took me into the delivery room. I could hear the conversation. "It's a placenta previa," Dr. McCaffrey explained to the intern, as they stood at the foot of the delivery table. "I had two choices. I could have sent Mary home to stay in bed 'til she comes to full term in six weeks . . . but that would be impossible with six youngsters at home. The fetal tone is strong and the size is viable, at least five and a half pounds, so I'm inducing."

Then he went on in his teaching voice, "A placenta previa in Latin means 'before the way'. It happens in about eight out of a thousand women Mary's age. The placenta isn't completely blocking the cervix so we don't have to consider doing a Caesarean." They talked as though I weren't even there. As the delivery advanced, they gave me some sodium pentothal. It was after nine o'clock that evening when I awakened in the recovery room.

"You have a healthy baby boy," the nurse was saying.

"Thank God," I mumbled in a sleepy whisper. "Where's the baby?"

"We put him in the incubator for the first twenty-four hours just as a precaution. He weighed five pounds, ten ounces, a good size for a preemie."

"We're gonna call him Peter"—I drifted back to sleep.

When Pete came the next day he questioned the name. "You really want to name him after me?"

We had considered the name each time we had a boy, but I had been turned off years before when Pete's mother would call my husband "Juneyah" (in her Boston accent) and worse yet, "Petey Jim." I could live with that now. Pete's great-grandfather, grandfather, and father had been Peter James McKenna, and this might be our last chance. There was a senior and junior; thus was born Peter James III.

Our home was hectic and happy. Jim, Elizabeth and Margaret were in the third, second and first grades at Assumption, John in kindergarten at Central, and I had three pre-schoolers. When I'd call the three who had to catch an early bus, all seven would come down to the kitchen. It was chaos. While I fixed their oatmeal and fruit juice, Jim would try to recite the seven gifts of the Holy Ghost, Elizabeth had to have a dollar for a new milk ticket, or Margaret wanted her name sewn on her mittens right now— "Sister said." When they left, I fed the younger children, and before nine o'clock Pete and I could have a peaceful cup of coffee. Then he had to open the shop for the day.

In the spring of 1958, some friends suggested we run away from home for a weekend. They were able to call on their grandmother to babysit, but ours were both working during the school year. I called the Peter Pan agency for their rates. "How many children do you have, Ma'am?"

"What difference does that make?" I knew I was trying to dodge.

"We have a basic rate for two children and an additional charge for each one after that. How many did you want cared for?"

"Se—ven," I said hesitatingly.

"Seven!" she yelled. "What do you do with that many children? I'm sorry, but I have no one who would accept that responsibility."

We were lucky to find a woman in the neighborhood who volunteered to help us. When we got back on Sunday night, she had her coat on and one foot out the door.

Each time we thought we were as busy as we could get, God "commissioned" us again. Two years after Peter's birth, we had another baby girl. Once again the score was even . . . four of each now, but nobody mentioned it. We named her Nellie, after three Irish great aunts. She was the queen of the roost—they all "mothered" her. Elizabeth sewed a bonnet and dress for her to wear home from the hospital. All the children helped with her christening party. The older children were able to babysit for a short time by now, another milestone for Pete and me. We could go to mass together, or just out for an ice cream cone without having to arrange for and pay a sitter.

Our house was bursting at the seams again; our kitchen barely held the ten of us around the table. When we invited two guests, we had to go to the basement to eat. The children were crowded into three small bedrooms. We added a family room off the kitchen and expanded an upstairs bedroom. Since they were popular at this time, we toyed with the idea of a fall-out shelter in the basement. We decided it would be a waste. By the time we stored eight hundred gallons of water and a two weeks' supply of groceries, there would be no room for us. Even if we survived the initial blast, we wouldn't survive each other.

Chapter XV

In May of '61 we had another addition. It seemed we were always "adding on", either rooms or kids. "Suffer the little children to come unto me and refuse them not." Paul Gerard arrived on May Day. St. Gerard is the patron saint of tired mothers, and I made a secret pact with him. We'd give his name to Paul if he'd turn off the fertility valve. Nine was fine! I was no longer challenged by my high school class motto: "Quitters never win; winners never quit!" Both Pete and I felt we had fulfilled our "commission." Now we needed the rest of His promise to give us "everything we asked in His Name."

Ten days before Paul was born, Pete thought I needed a change of scenery. A friend was going to Chicago to visit her husband and she was afraid to fly. "Mary will go with you," Pete volunteered. "She loves to fly."

That was the weekend of the worst snowstorm of the season, and in Chicago it can cripple the entire transportation system. I was stranded at Midway airport—no planes were leaving. When a bus was to shuttle us to O'Hare, it got stuck in the snow. The other passengers, who were all male, dug it out and I kept studying each man to see who might be a good mid-wife. At O'Hare the ticket agent looked at my bulging front and asked how "far along" I was. When I told him I was due in a week, he wouldn't let me on the plane.

"We have over two hundred planes up there, and we can't take a chance."

My friend couldn't get in from Chicago Heights anyway, so I spent the night in a motel near the airport. We got home on Monday; Paul was born the following Sunday.

In my Christmas letter of 1961, I said, "Paul is what every busy mother dreams of. He just stays in his play pen and smiles until someone has time to take care of him. I hope he stays this way for awhile 'cause I'm turning gray keeping up with Nellie. She's been in'the terrible twos' stage for almost a year and she won't be two until next month."

Jim was eleven when our ninth child was born. If a time and motion expert were to analyze our production system, he would have to admit we didn't waste either one. It didn't seem unmanageable to us though. The babies came fast, but not all at once. We were geared for the nursery set. I never stopped making formula or washing diapers between births. Pete did all the baths, and as long as he was down on his knees he didn't mind scrubbing two or six. It was a production line every night, but besides sharing the same bath water, the children shared their good night prayers and their daddy's wild bedtime stories.

Large families were common in our community during the fifties, and we were not aware of any disadvantages we suffered because of our children. Eight couples who were our good friends could gather at a picnic with sixty-three children! We had peer support.

Another Christmas tradition Pete and I have helped keep alive for about twenty years is our church's caroling party. When we started in the middle fifties, we had an outside Nativity scene in front of our Marian Shop, so the last stop would be our house to put the infant in the crib, and have hot chocolate and sloppy Joes.

About thirty or forty adults, including my two aunts and uncles, meet at our church parking lot and begin the evening by singing for the nuns and priests. We have a list of the elderly and ill people in the parish and our parade of cars moves from one house to the next. We have had a hard time keeping back the tears as we've sung to friends with terminal cancer. One house-bound lady and her husband always welcome us all into their house for a glass of wine and then we sing extra loud and extra long.

One year we rented a sleigh to make the caroling party more authentic—also more expensive. We have never canceled because of the weather, but when it gets to be a minus forty windchill, we know who are the dedicated carolers.

Chapter XVI

If I could choose the "best years of my life"—without having to live them over again—I would choose the late nineteen-fifties and early sixties. We were enjoying each stage of each child's growth. They were busy years of togetherness. Our family seemed closest when we all needed each other.

The older ones helped with the housework and with the smaller children when I was busy in the shop or in the hospital having a baby. Elizabeth would make thirty-five sandwiches on Sunday night and freeze them for school lunches. We worked together in the shop, Pete and I, and the children. Jim had a paper route, Elizabeth cleaned a neighbor's bathroom every week, and Margaret was a "mug washer" at the root beer stand. When I mentioned the Depression to our children, they jokingly asked, "Which one, yours or ours?"

Although our business was flourishing, our expenses were, too. There were orthodontist bills, music lessons, tuition, doctor and hospital bills (we could never join a "group"). Our son, Peter, had a rare mastoidectomy when he was three. John fell into a newly cemented basement and had a compound fracture. Because there was no room in the hospital, I had to take him home when the anesthesia wore off. Mary Catherine swallowed furniture polish and had to have her stomach pumped. We paid our obstetrician twenty-five dollars a month, until one hundred and twenty-five dollars was paid. The dentist was a year-around thirty dollars a month. Our additions to the house and shop took lump sums of two to four thousand dollars, our profit from a good Christmas season.

We bought clothes at rummage sales, wore hand-me-downs, ate day-old bread, powdered milk and casseroles, and I gave ten home haircuts every few weeks. Although we had a balanced diet, we skimped on our budget to have money for our summer vacations and travel. Summers would have been unbearable with the long hot days, prolonged by daylight-saving time. Our upstairs bedrooms were too hot to sleep in before ten o'clock so we had tired, cranky kids until it cooled off. If we had a long hot spell, we all took blankets and pillows and slept on the floor of the air-conditioned shop.

On Saturday night when all the children were bathed and ready for bed, their Sunday outfits all laid out, and prayers and bedtime stories finished, Pete and I would sink into bed and try to catch a fast night's sleep. We knew that early Sunday morning they'd all come into our bed. It was the only morning we didn't have to open the door that led to the shop. The kids loved to snuggle under our covers as Pete and I tried to extend our arms around five or seven or all nine of them. More than once our bed collapsed.

We played together; every summer we had something to look forward to. In 1959 we went to Big Island on Lake Minnetonka, twenty minutes from home. This island is owned by the State of Minnesota and is dedicated to the Veterans Administration to be used by veterans and their families, at a nominal cost. We packed our bedding, swimming gear, and a few changes of clothes and drove to the dock in Excelsior. A married couple managed the project; he was the pilot on the ferry back and forth to the island twice a day, and she supervised the kitchen. We went with two other families, each of whom also had a half dozen kids, and we stretched the ferry to capacity.

The biggest attraction of this island vacation for us tired mothers was that the price included the meals. When the bell rang everyone raced to the dining hall where one of the other fathers and I pushed a cart down the cafeteria line and filled a dozen plates with the delicious food for our youngsters. It was heavenly—no groceries to buy, no hot stove, no dirty dishes. The fact that there were no bathrooms in the cabin and we had to bathe in a community shower didn't dim our appreciation of our week off.

That same summer, when Elizabeth was nine years old, she flew to Washington to visit her grandparents. As the oldest girl, she had earned a special treat, and the grandparents could give her some individual attention and love. Maybe it was the poem she wrote for me on Mother's Day that earned the trip for her.

MY MOTHER

My mother is an angel
Come down to spread her wings,
My mother is an image
Of every glorious thing.
My mother is patience,
My mother is love,
My mother is a treasure
That came from up above.
I love my mother dearly,
I know we couldn't part,
Because she is MY mother
I love her with all my heart.
Elizabeth McKenna.

When Pete and I saw her off at the airport, we had qualms about our little girl going off by herself and transferring planes in Detroit. We needn't have worried. The airline stewardesses were her personal escorts until they handed her to her grandparents in Washington.

In 1960 we took the oldest five children to Washington and Boston to the BVA convention. We visited many friends and relatives along the way; it took a lot of nerve to write and ask if the seven of us could drop in. By this time all the children were old enough to appreciate visiting the White House, the Smithsonian and Arlington Cemetery in Washington. They also enjoyed visiting Plymouth Rock, Old Ironsides, Paul Revere's house, Lexington and Concord, and a clam bake near Boston.

One lady in Concord stood on "the rude bridge that arched the flood . . ." where "once the embattled farmers stood" and yelled to her little boy underneath the bridge, "I didn't haul you all the way from Arizona to Massachusetts to play with a frog." Historical monuments aren't for everybody.

With our oldest four into Scouting it was inevitable that Mom and Dad get into it, too. Pete became a Merit Badge Counselor for Citizenship. This was as close as he had come to using his degree in American History. He also was an assistant camper. The troop went on weekend over-nights regardless of the weather. Pete had entertained our boys with stories of his Army days when he slept out in the open on the snow. Twenty years later sleeping in a tent in minus ten degree weather held no thrills for him, but he went anyway. One time his cheeks turned white and his prosthetic eyes froze in the sockets.

When Jim went to summer camp for two weeks, we loaded the car with a borrowed tent and camping gear, food, mosquito repellent, and kids, to meet him for the weekend. The mosquitoes were mammoth, and the ants were legion. Several families we knew came up that same weekend so we had tent-raising bees, community dining, singing, and commiserating. The smile on Jim's face when we arrived and the outdoor mass on Sunday morning were the only redeeming features of the weekend. We had only three sleeping bags and two car seats for the seven of us and with the temperature dipping to forty-six degrees we were not sold on the joys of camping.

Elizabeth and Margaret were Girl Scouts looking for a troop leader. When someone asked me if I'd be one, I declined graciously. "I have nine children, you know."

"Bernie is willing to be a co-leader. She has ten kids!" What could I say?

When Pete's folks celebrated their forty-fifth wedding anniversary in Washington, we were there. "Pop", as we called his father, had suffered a stroke and a heart attack within the year, so we didn't need much prodding to go.

My parents had just retired, my father from the bank and my mother from teaching. They came in and ran our business, plus babysitting their nine grandchildren. It was an act of love. Pete and I enjoyed six days of adult company. We went on to Princeton, New Jersey, where my brother and his wife were waiting with their week-old baby girl; we were to be the godparents.

When we were having our annual babies, Dr. McCaffrey jokingly suggested an alternative to sex.

"Go fly a kite, instead," he told Pete. Our friends chided him about it; he was the only person who could fly one at night.

After Paul was born, I thought exercise would be good for both Pete and me. But what kind? We couldn't join a softball league together, or golf, or play tennis. For Father's Day, we gave Pete a tandem bicycle. It seemed the perfect solution, until we tried riding it together. Tandem bikes are made for the man to be in front. We were disappointed. "Pete, either you've got to find a tall wife or have this frame cut down," I suggested.

"It'd be simpler to change the bike."

I called several machine shops and finally found a man who understood what I wanted. He was from Germany and had lots of experience with bicycles. I took the tandem to his shop where he lowered the rod, the seat and the handle bars in front so I could reach the ground. When Pete and I went out to pick up the remodeled bike, the man asked Peter where he had been injured.

"Kassel, Germany."

The man swallowed hard, looked at me, then at Pete. There were tears in his eyes. "My home was in Kassel. I was fighting there, too." There was no charge for his work on our bicycle.

Chapter XVII

What ever happened to "Easter outfits?" Whatever did, was one of the better residuals of the hippie fashion revolution. In the fifties and early sixties I started a month before holy week to line up outfits for each child: patent leather shoes, dresses, bonnets, and gloves for the girls; sport jackets, white shirts and ties, trousers, and shoes for the boys. Many of these could be "handed down" because they never wore out. From my own Depression Days, I couldn't shake two hang-ups that irritated my children: saving clothes "for good", and buying clothes "to grow into." By the time we had all nine children outfitted, Pete and I usually settled for a dry-cleaning job on ours.

Easter was a busy season in our Marian Shop—Lenten reading, parish missions, and hundreds of second graders making their First Communion. But Easter Sunday was Family Day. Early in the morning, Pete would go outside and put a half-eaten carrot on the step and then ring the doorbell. "Hey, kids, you just missed him! Look, quick, you might see his tail around the corner!"

The youngsters would bound down the stairs to look for their Easter baskets. It was happy bedlam. I was relieved when the older children didn't believe in the Easter Bunny anymore so they could help me dye the eggs and hide the baskets. My special treat for Pete was always a Fanny Farmer chocolate cream egg.

By the time all eleven of us were snapped and zippered into our Easter finery, there would usually be one or two arguments.

"Nellie won't let me comb her hair!"

"Joe won't give me my tie. Just 'cause he wore it last year, he thinks it's his!"

"Margaret's taking candy to church in her purse."

Pete could usually calm all the ripples by singing, "Don your Easter bonnet, with all the frills upon it. You'll be the grandest lady in the Easter Parade."

After forty days of reading the Stations of the Cross after dinner, going to mass every day, and giving up candy or desserts, we were all ready for the Resurrection. The music, the bells, the Easter lilies, and triumphal liturgy were a welcome change from the purple draped statues.

Each spring we had a new First Communicant who could join us at the altar to share the Eucharistic meal. When Paul's turn came, his sister Nellie asked, "Who's going to hold our seat for us? We won't be able to find our way back to our pew without him there."

One Easter Sunday when Jim drove his own car to church, he took Paul with him after mass, but we were unaware of this. While we searched in vain, this same loving sister piped up, "It's just like when the Holy Family lost Jesus. Let's come back and look for him in three days!"

My big treat on Easter was going to a restaurant for breakfast. We usually had to split up into two booths or tables, and the older children enjoyed being on their own. After we had coached them that there was a dollar limit, it was embarrassing when one of them would holler across the room, "Can I have the dollar twenty-five plate if I pay the difference?" Invariably someone would order a side dish of sausage or orange juice and throw off the whole budget!

After breakfast we would drive over to the Visitation Convent in St. Paul to visit our cousin, Sister Teresa. Even though the nuns had a girls' school, the Visitation Convent was cloistered, and usually we had to visit through the grilled walls. On Easter Sunday they opened the doors and the world came in to disrupt their quiet, sheltered life. The McKenna tribe did their share. The sisters always had candy for the children, and then the younger nuns would take them to the gym to play volleyball, basketball, or gymnastics while Pete and I visited with Sister Teresa. Although she was in her eighties, she was vibrant and interested in everything that was going on in the outside world. I always enjoyed hearing her tell of her first time out of the convent walls in forty years.

"You know, when I entered the convent back in aught eight," she'd start reminiscing, "there were horse-drawn ice wagons, cobblestone roads, and gas lights."

When she became the "Mother Superior" she had to travel to Mobile, Alabama. On the way to the train depot she asked the driver to detour a little so she could see what had happened to her beloved St. Paul. She was shocked by all the traffic, the neon lights, and the large stores and office buildings. "Glory be to God, I'll be glad to get back to the convent!" she'd told the driver.

"You should come out for a peek now, Sister," we'd tell her. "There's six lanes of traffic, shopping centers all over the suburbs, and television antennae sprouting out of every roof in the city."

Until she was immobilized by arthritis, Sister Teresa would usually play the piano for the children; "Kitten on the Keys" was their favorite. Shortly after we celebrated her diamond jubilee with her, she went home to Heaven. Our children missed her when she died. Even though there was an eighty-year age difference, she could bridge the four-generation gap.

Easter was never quite the same.

Chapter XVIII

When we finally quit washing diapers after thirteen years, we decided we'd rent a lake cottage for a week. I had shied away from this kind of vacation because I thought cooking, cleaning, and laundry were hard enough chores at home. I wanted no part of doing difficult jobs under difficult conditions. Now, without having to tote a diaper pail we felt free.

Our friends, Bill and Lois Andersen, who had five children plus their niece, rented the cabin three doors down from us. When we set out our first community meal with fifteen children some passers-by inquired, "Is this a Bible Camp?"

It rained the first three days. Early Monday morning, we sent a note to the Andersens' cabin. "We're desperate. There will be a talent show at seven o'clock tonight, and your family is invited to participate. Don't hide your light under a bushel!"

While there have been more professional productions, I've never seen one more enjoyable. Pete sang "Harrigan" and played his harmonica. He and I did the "elephant walk." Our children hummed on kazoos made from cigarette papers over a comb, and played other adapted kitchen musical instruments. The Andersens came as circus characters. Bill was the Strong Man; Lois, who was six months pregnant, was the Fat Lady; and their youngsters were fortune tellers, tight rope walkers, belly dancers, and midgets. The third rainy day Lois and I decided to drive into town to the laundromat and let the men babysit. Needless to say, the kids spent the day in the rain.

When a cousin was getting married, our relatives put a cookbook together with recipes from each of us. I included directions for:

BREAKFAST FOR SIX, EIGHT, TEN, OR MORE

Turn off alarm. Get up immediately. It's worse if you wait.

Say morning prayers: "Good morning, God" or "Good God, morning!" depending on your frame of mind.

Wake up school children. Pre-schoolers will bounce out; others will growl at you.

Brace yourself with warmed-over black coffee.

Clean up mess from popcorn and sandwich making from night before.

Set out boxes of cereal, juice, milk, toast, etc. Don't pour anything; they probably won't take time to eat.

Sit down and write excuses for absences, homework that was done but lost, and girl scout permits.

Stand in doorway for goodbye kisses and smiles. Don't be surprised if you don't get either one.

Run out with forgotten lunches.

Take out curlers, put on lipstick, and sexy robe. Smile when hubby comes out to eat.

During the middle thirties when my aunts and uncles were raising their families in Minneapolis, they started several traditions which have survived for over forty years. Our family is fortunate that we meet for happy occasions as well as funerals.

A mid-summer picnic on the Fourth of July at Minnehaha Park was the highlight of the season during the Depression. Everyone packed hot dogs and kids into an old Chevie or onto the streetcar and gathered near the deer pens at the Park. There were ball games and races for every age.

I joined the group when I was in nurses' training in the forties—I needed to be part of a family even though I had left home several years before. Everyone was welcome at these picnics, and by the time we all brought a friend, we numbered three dozen.

When the second generation got into the baby boom, there were too many toddlers to watch at a public park. A cousin who had a

walk-out basement adjacent to a playground invited us to use
their house one year, and we've been going back ever since.
When we had our nine children, playpen, teeterbabe, high chair,
potty seat, wet wash cloth, and picnic basket packed in our station wagon, we looked like Pa and Ma Kettle. More than once we
left the picnic minus one child. Someone always brought the stray
one home to us.

My Aunt Agnes was born on the Fourth of July and was as
musical as George M. Cohan. At our picnics, she played the piano
in the basement, and all the youngsters carried flags and marched
in and out of the house to patriotic tunes. We celebrated her
birthday along with America's.

Birthday parties were another tradition. We, with our aunts and
cousins, had a party for each birthday until there were so many
we had to have a monthly party for two or three birthdays. We
were fortunate that most of the women worked in hospitals and
could get a day off in the middle of the week. We started out
giving birthday presents, but finally settled for fifty cents from
everyone—the birthday celebrants could buy their own gifts.

The third annual family affair was the Christmas party. It
started in Aunt Rosie's basement, but again, when we all had
children, we had to move to different accommodations. We rented
Morris Hall on Lake Street for ten dollars. Two small rooms
upstairs had two essentials, a kitchen and a piano. We brought
gifts for the children, and one of the men donned a Santa Claus
suit to distribute them. A cousin made a piñata for the small
children, and it was bedlam when it broke. Our pot-luck supper
was ill-planned and shanty Irish until one of my half-
Scandinavian cousins organized it into a savory smorgasbord.
Our Christmas parties grew to over a hundred relatives, and we
had to rent larger and larger halls. One year a little black boy
joined our party, and everyone thought he was someone's friend.
When there wasn't a present for him, we asked him who he came
with. "I came by myself," he said. "It looked like you were
having a good time, so I came in."

Santa found a gift for him.

Chapter XIX

On January 25, 1959, when Pope John unexpectedly, and some thought jokingly, announced that he would call together the Vatican Council, he had no idea what he was doing to Pete and me. Our Marian Shop was selling religious articles and sacramentals that had been used by Catholics for centuries.

When the Council document on the Sacred Liturgy was completed in December of 1963, the bottom fell out of the missal business. Even the publishers didn't know exactly when and what the new missals would offer. There was no market for the obsolete ones.

Then the saints began to topple. No one wanted to buy a statue of St. Christopher if he was no longer canonized.

Using the vernacular made the liturgy more meaningful and encouraged lay participation. Catholics began using more personal and spontaneous prayer. There was less rote, fewer litanies, novenas, and rosaries.

All these changes in the church affected our business—slowly and adversely. But Vatican II was not the only reason for our business and family decline. God is providential; we needed a change in our life style.

Our home was in a commercial zone and other businesses had built right up to our door. We no longer had the privacy of our back yard. Because of our location, the real-estate taxes had tripled in ten years, and commercial property cannot be homesteaded. The eldest children had reached their teens and there was more activity behind the scenes than we could subdue because of "the customers." It was embarrassing for Pete when he was waiting on a customer and they both could hear, "I did the dishes for you last night and you always get out of all the work!"

"Oh yeah? You said you'd do them for me if I let you wear my sweater."

Our kids complained about the family having a business phone with their calls limited to three minutes. At that time we thought only doctors had a "children's phone" listed in the telephone directory.

Pete was getting cabin fever being confined twenty-four hours a day while the ten of us were coming and going. With the decline in business from 1963 to 1965 he had lots of time on his hands; even reading his Talking Books became tiresome. We prayed that he would find something to do outside our home, but there were no job possibilities for him. He developed various pains in his head, stomach, and prostate and was hospitalized several times. He complained to the doctors about not being able to sleep, but much of the time when he listened to his recording machine during the day he'd drop off for a nap, and consequently he wasn't tired at night. The doctors prescribed tranquilizers and sleeping pills, and gradually Pete became dependent on pills to get through the monotonous days and long nights.

As I saw what was happening to Pete, our family, and our business, I became irritable and depressed. I am a worrier, however useless it is, and my mind was preoccupied with the children, their school performance, their discipline, and the financial strain we were experiencing. I needed a change of scenery.

In October of 1963 my bridge club ran away from home leaving forty-four children motherless. The Burlington Northern Railroad had a weekend excursion to Chicago for seventeen dollars. That included two nights at a hotel. We played bridge in the club car all the way. In Chicago, we must have looked like a bunch of 4H girls on their first visit to the big city. The hotel detective had to tell us to keep our doors closed "for our own protection." We reacted with motherly concern when some young sailors who'd had too much to drink asked us to join their party. As we roamed through one of the vast drugstores gathering souvenirs for our families and making small talk as though we were at home at the corner grocer's, a man approached us with the air of an old cosmopolitan and warned us, "Watch your purses, ladies—this is the pickpocket capital of the world! They come here from both coasts to learn the trade."

After I made my purchases, including a pint of Seagram's V.O. for my husband, I stood in line at the checkout counter clutching my purse and my merchandise with guarded eyes. Finally I said to my companions, "I'm getting a little shaky in here."

The gentleman behind me, another veteran of the Windy City, tried to reassure me, "I've had the shakes myself, lady. You'll feel a lot better after you've had a swig from that bottle!"

When Jim graduated from the eighth grade in 1964 no Catholic family worth the "stars in their crown" would consider a public high school for their children. That was second-class citizenship. Because the competition was stiff, Jim was not accepted in the Twin Cities' Catholic high schools, but that did not deter us from our "obligation." We enrolled him in a boarding school in Madison, Wisconsin. We figured the six hundred dollars of tuition would just about feed him at home. My brother was teaching at the University of Wisconsin that year, and we knew Jim would be a part of their family. We rationalized that being away from us might be good for him. The eleven of us had been close and maybe a fourteen-year-old boy needed breathing space from his eight younger sisters and brothers.

It was a long, unhappy year for him and for us. Frequently we'd get a call collect, "Mom, we're off next Monday. Can I come home?" What could I say? It meant sending him ten dollars for bus fare, but it was worth it for all of us. The girls told me later that each time he came home he wished he'd get sick so he wouldn't have to go back. The next year we regained our senses and enrolled him at Richfield High School, an excellent public school two blocks away. We learned that Catholic high schools are not for everyone.

Elizabeth and Margaret, on the other hand, attended Regina High School, run by Dominican sisters. It was right for them.

They both worked to help with their tuition—Libby (we gave up
on her formal name when Nellie couldn't pronounce it) worked in
a real-estate office, and Margaret for Kentucky Fried Chicken. By
paying monthly installments, we were able to cover their expenses.

While Pete was escaping reality with drugs, and I was having a
"closet" nervous breakdown from trying to cope, our children
suffered the consequences. We had sibling rivalry (commonly
called family fights), petty stealing, school failures, and abnormal
bed-wetting. When I told Pete's doctor at the Veterans Hospital
what was happening, he prescribed family counseling. "For us?"
I asked, unbelievingly. I thought only broken homes needed
counseling. Ours was not a broken home, but it was slowly breaking up.

"Yes," he explained patiently, "the whole family is sick and
needs healing."

Our first encounter was a fiasco. The children—in fact all of
us—were embarrassed, and reacted by being silent or silly. The
counselor had difficulty remembering each kid's name, much less
what was bothering him. Several times the two youngest wandered away and got lost.

We went once a week for several months, and the sessions
became more open. We learned the individual needs and hopes
and hurts of each member of the family and tried to do something
about it. I guess the group therapy helped; years later we were
even able to joke about it. We decided to change our life style—
we would sell our home and shop and move to a residential neighborhood. Pete had no prospects for another job, but we'd move
anyway. We couldn't go on as we were, and we felt the Good
Lord was steering us, so He'd have the answers.

Chapter XX

On the first Sunday of April, 1965, we packed all the kids in the station wagon after mass, and started off for Browerville to surprise Grandma John on her sixty-fifth birthday. We had a beautifully decorated cake on the front seat between Pete and me. It was a rainy day, and as we started our trip with the usual rosary, the car windows got steamed up. Everyone was breathing.

I didn't see the police car following me for a mile—from the fifty mile zone to the thirty-five. I was still going forty-seven when he stopped me. As he asked, "How fast were you going?" I panicked. I remembered the other two times in the past year. Being preoccupied with family problems and driving a car are not compatible. I had learned to drive as a necessity when I began dating Pete. Since then I've been steering the wheel ten to fifteen thousand miles every year, and I always considered myself a good driver. I had never had a serious accident. The previous summer as I had driven Elizabeth over to her sewing lessons, late, I had seen a flashing red light behind me. I had slowed down to let him pass. When his car was abreast of mine I had heard a loud snarly voice roar, "Pull over, lady!"

"Me?" I had gestured toward myself with a questioning look.

"Yes, you," as he pulled in behind me. He had walked up to my window and asked, "How fast were you driving?"

"I-I-d-don't know. I didn't look at the speedometer."

"You were driving forty-two miles an hour in a thirty-five mile zone. Let me see your driver's license. . . . Take it out," he had added, as I flashed the card in my billfold. He had taken my license and gone back to the squad car. Elizabeth and I watched nervously as he talked into his car radio. It had seemed to take forever. It was like waiting for a stay of execution. When he had come back to my car, he handed me a ticket. "You have three days to pay this fine. You are to appear in the Bloomington Traffic Court on July 16. Y'better watch your speedometer from now on."

I had been tempted to say, "But, officer, I was in a hurry to—" but he had gone.

A few months later I had been driving out to a lumber yard and trying to keep up the prayers of a nine-hour novena when I saw another flashing light. The same routine, only this time radar had caught me. You don't argue with that. I'd been driving forty-five in a thirty-five zone. The fine was larger, and I had to go over to the State Highway Department to explain my speeding problem. I had been the only woman in the line-up. When I told the man that "everyone drives over the speed limit during the rush hour without getting a ticket," it didn't help my cause. Both times I'd been stopped it was mid-morning, and I was beginning to think the police had a vendetta out against housewives.

"Let me see your license!" I was jerked back to the present.

"But, officer, please. You don't know what this means. They told me if I got another speeding ticket they'd take my license away!"

"That shoulda made you more careful than ever," he said unsympathetically.

"But don't you see, I'm the only driver for all eleven of us."

"You shoulda thought of that, lady. Here's your ticket."

I was in tears, but they didn't help either. We turned the car around and drove home quietly, in no partying mood. I was glad my mother didn't know we were coming, because I would hate to have called to explain what her forty-three-year-old daughter had done. We ate her birthday cake glumly.

For getting three speeding tickets, I had to surrender my license for thirty days, pay a fifty dollar fine, or spend ten days in jail. (I would have served time, but by this time Pete was in the hospi-

tal.) I had to take the written test and road test again, and go on
risk insurance for three years. I have read of drunken drivers who
have killed people getting no more than this. For someone who
was depressed already, this predicament was devastating. While
Pete was hospitalized, I had been taking the two pre-schoolers,
Nellie and Paul, to a baby sitter while I worked in the shop. I
couldn't drive them over, so I put one on the back seat of the
tandem bicycle and the other in the front basket and off I pedalled
ten blocks to the sitter.

It was a difficult month, but neighbors and friends helped us
with rides for groceries, errands, and church. The financial strain
of the risk insurance went on for three years. The lesson I learned
lasted forever. I always watch the speedometer and the rear view
mirror.

Real estate wasn't moving in 1965. Especially a five bedroom
home in a commercial zone with a shop attached. I had driven by
a Cape Cod colonial house four blocks away for over ten years
and admired the setting. Now it was for sale. The yard was huge
with about twenty oak trees, and I fell in love with the place. It
was just like Scarlett O'Hara's father said, "To anyone with a
drop of Irish blood in them, the land is just like their mother."
The rest of the family looked at it more realistically. The house
was old and too small for our family, the oak trees would shed
bushels of leaves to be raked, and even mowing all the grass
would be a chore. At that time we had many helping hands and
none of these objections seemed insurmountable to me.

We bought the house, and the children helped us move during
their Christmas vacation. Now we owned two houses. I should
say we shared the second one with the bank and the previous
owner who took a contract for deed.

Throughout January, February, and March we sold the remaining stock of the Marian Shop. It was sad to witness the death of
our first business venture, but Pete was relieved to be out of it. He
applied for a vending stand through the State Services for the
Blind, and they accepted him for training. There was no promise
of being placed when he finished the course, however.

Meanwhile the bills came in. The taxes, insurance and heating
bills from our unoccupied house came to three hundred dollars

per month. We had two electric bills, one at commercial rates, and the house we moved into needed rewiring with the heavy load we put on the circuit.

We had lived on Pete's disability compensation before, but with the extra expense we were finding it difficult. There were no openings in the vending stand program, so rather than have both of us home stewing about our finances, I offered to go back to nursing. Pete thought it a good idea, too. He was still addicted to brain-numbing pills. He had devious ways of getting them and hiding them, and of course, denying that he had any problem. The smell of one certain capsule permeated from his lungs, and it turned me from him physically. "My God", I prayed, "what is happening to him, to us, to our marriage?"

Chapter XXI

It had been almost eighteen years since "Miss John" left Mt. Alto Veterans' Hospital on a temporary leave to get married. The hospital world had changed considerably since then. The only department I hadn't lost touch with was obstetrics!

Methodist Hospital was offering a one-month refresher course in November of 1966. I paid the twenty-five dollar fee and enrolled. Getting out with all nine of the school kids by eight o'clock in the morning was no mean feat, but we managed. There were two nurses in the class who were even older than I. The Public Health doctor boosted my sagging ego when he said, "You older nurses should never feel that you're not needed. You have an intangible quality that younger nurses don't learn any more—the 'pillow fluffing technique.'"

After a month of concentrated nursing instructions, I felt a sense of accomplishment as I received my certificate. I was once again qualified to "practice" nursing—and that's what it would be.

I began my "practice" at St. Mary's hospital when a dear friend, Sister Margaret Clare, got me a job two days a week as a "float." I replaced nurses on their days off or helped out when they were understaffed. Everyone at the hospital and at home was patient as I got back into the routine. It was a good feeling for an old nurse to get back into uniform—I was proud to wear my University of Minnesota cap and pin once more.

One of the fringe benefits of working at St. Mary's Hospital was that I could renew my friendship with Father Kelly, a multiple sclerosis victim whom I had met when Peter was born there in 1958. Any time I was near Room 547, I'd stop by for his blessing and his blarney.

After Francis Paschal Kelly was ordained a Dominican priest in 1933, he had come to Minneapolis to be an assistant at Holy Rosary Church. At twenty-nine he was a handsome man, six feet tall, dark curly hair, with penetrating blue eyes and black bushy eyebrows. He had come full of pastoral zeal and love for people, but he had only one year of ministry before serious signs of multiple sclerosis began to appear: weakness, uncoordination, and paralysis. Within ten years, he was confined to a wheelchair. He spent twelve years in an upstairs room at the rectory of Holy Rosary Church, and from here he was a zealous minister to his people. He counseled, instructed, baptized, married, and even buried from his wheelchair.

In 1956 when he no longer could sit upright or get around by himself he entered St. Mary's Hospital. No one realized that this would be his home for the next nineteen years. Each year a little more of his independence was stripped from him; when I met him he could still move his left hand, his head a little, and his mouth a whole lot. He never lost his sense of humor and he had a new story for each visitor.

Father Kelly was a man full of contradictions. Although he was celibate, he was a matchmaker and family counselor. He loved to get people together, and he wanted to be a part of everyone's family. He was thrilled with new babies, children came for his blessing on their First Communion Day, and nurses came back in their bridal gowns to share their day with him. He always remembered to ask about husbands, grandparents, maiden aunts, everyone.

Although he couldn't move an inch he was a travel agent. Whenever he met a person for the first time, he'd ask where they were from. He invariably knew someone from the area and the conversation took off from there. He stored this geographical data so that if a friend were traveling to any city or country in the world, Father Kelly had someone for them to meet. He had a fantastic memory for names and places and he made everyone feel special because he remembered.

Although he couldn't applaud, he loved show people. He had a photo gallery of his "pin-up girls"—Helen Hayes, Hildegarde, Carmel Quinn, Mary Tyler Moore, Jane Wyatt, and Fran Allison among them. Dennis Day, Pat O'Brien, Jimmy Durante, Dick Van Dyke, and Fred Waring all came to his hospital room. At their first visit they came believing they were doing him a favor, but soon realized as they came again and again that it was to have their own spirits lifted.

Although he couldn't move a muscle, he loved to watch other people in action. He once said, "I have a nineteen-year-old body inside me that wants to come out." His first love was baseball. He had followed the Minnesota Twins when they were the Washington Senators and never missed a game on the radio or television. Whenever Pete came in to visit with him, they reminisced about old Clark Griffith; they were Pete's "home team" too. They also talked about Catholic University and the Dominican House of Studies. We had gone to mass there when we lived in Washington. Athletes from every major league team, baseball as well as football and hockey, stopped in for his blessing.

Father Kelly was chaplain, social worker, engineer, confidante and friend to both the great and the not so great. He had volunteer aides for each day of the week and they all felt privileged to be one of his "pushers." After mass in the morning, they would wheel him to the lobby, where he read the newspaper and held court from his specially built high wheel chair. When he and his pusher had picked up the list of new patients to see if he should add them to his daily rounds, he rode through the halls and gave his blessing to those requesting it and a hello to anyone who looked in need of cheering. Many people credited him and his powerful prayers for their recoveries, but he insisted it was the power of God; he was only His PR man.

The hospital staff, his family of doctors, nurses, aides, orderlies, housekeepers and tradesmen were all devoted to him. They equipped his room with every engineering device that could make his life more enjoyable: keys to press for his television and telephone, prism glasses and mirrors to reflect images, and amplifiers to ease his failing voice.

Each time I stopped in to visit him he would have me open his can of candy and take a piece for each of our children. He had an inexhaustible supply of these treats. After I knelt for his blessing, he had a twinkle in his Irish eyes as he said, "God love ye, Mary darlin'."

Thus the days and weeks and months and seasons passed. After nineteen years at St. Mary's Hospital his tired body was completely locked in. His eyesight was going, he couldn't swallow, and even his fantastic memory was failing him. This hurt. He was ready to go Home, and he asked his friends to pray that it would be soon. On February 7, 1975, Father Paschal Kelly went to his Father's House. He had fought the good fight, he had finished the course, he had kept the faith. As he lay in state in full Dominican habit at his beloved Holy Rosary Church (the shoes were a shock!), his many, many friends came to say goodbye. Each would remember that special something he had going with Father Kelly.

Chapter XXII

As I raced around giving baths, medications, and TLC at the hospital, I could almost forget my problems at home. But not quite. During the Christmas vacation that year Pete took the boys out to try their new toboggan. He didn't know the hill was a ski jump until it was too late. He went sailing through the air after the toboggan hit a tree and landed on his left hand—the one he injured during WWII. When they X-rayed at the VA Hospital, they found not only the bones of the hand broken, but also the wires that had been inserted almost twenty years ago. The pain was excruciating. It was like reopening an old wound. The orthopedic surgeon had to rebuild his hand, and Pete was in the hospital until April. They were difficult months. I worked two days a week which made a difficult physical load, but the mental anguish was worse. I knew the doctors would be prescribing more drugs for Pete, and although I had notices put on his chart to prevent it, with the constantly changing staff it was impossible to keep ahead. Like an alcoholic, he didn't think he had a problem.

Then the Lord came through again.

In May of 1967, a month after Pete came out of the hospital, he was offered the vending stand at the Minneapolis City Hall. With much trepidation in both our minds, he began work. He had not traveled alone since his streetcar days at the University of Minnesota. He had not handled the bookkeeping aspect of our gift shop. He had not even gotten up early in the morning. It was going to be a whole new way of life for all of us.

Because his stand opened at seven o'clock in the morning, Pete got up at five. I am non-functioning at that hour, so we worked out

93

a system whereby he wouldn't need my droopy presence. With a few preparations by me the night before, he was able to make his own breakfast. He came to enjoy this peaceful hour alone in the kitchen. It gave him a chance to organize his day and keep up with the news on the radio.

After a few days of riding the bus downtown, he became acquainted with passengers who were walking the two blocks to the City Hall and were happy to "give him an arm."

Learning the physical set-up of his vending stand with a dozen kind of cigars, twenty some brands of cigarettes, hundreds of candy items, plus the soft drinks, ice creams, and sandwiches was a challenge. He also had to be alert to traffic noises when he traveled, to recognize voices of customers, and to add up long columns of figures in his head.

Pete had an orderly mind and a good memory, but he realized that he couldn't keep on top of things if he were constantly tranquilized. One lost weekend convinced him that he needed help to overcome his dependence on drugs if he wanted to succeed in his new business. He went on his own to an AA meeting and convinced them that a drug dependency was as debilitating as alcohol. They accepted him for membership and worked with him for over a year—until the national organization vetoed accepting non-alcoholic members. By this time Pete, despite several "slippages", had recovered. God had blessed us again.

For ten years Pete enjoyed the camaraderie of the police, the politicians, and the prisoners at the city hall. He was on a first-name basis with the mayor, the chief of police, and judges, as well as the elevator operator, the paper boy, and the chronic drunks.

Whenever someone tried to pawn off a one-dollar bill for a twenty, Pete could count on a couple of big policemen to come to his aid.

He was happy at his work. He dispensed a little homespun philosophy and Irish songs, along with his sales. Many city hall customers talked to him about their gripes and problems. "When they hear me sing, they wonder if I'm sober," he quipped. "I sing 'cause I'm happy."

He had good rapport with his fellow blind vendors, and was elected president of their state organization.

Chapter XXIII

In the latter half of the sixties and early seventies the world, the Church, authority in general, and our family in particular was falling apart. With as many as six teenagers at once each "doing his own thing" it could be disastrous, and sometimes was. Previous to this time we had the usual discipline problems:

"Mommy, Daddy! Jimmy's out of bed" was a sing-song that we heard nightly.

"John took all my Halloween candy!"

"Nellie colored all over my catechism book!"

"Joe hit me first!"

"Make Margaret clean her half of the room!"

These annoyances were dealt with without much difficulty. It reminded me of my parents' simplistic method of discipline. They had a little wine glass for each of us, and every Sunday we each started out with four navy beans in our glass. For every good thing we did, a bean was added; for every transgression, a bean was taken away. At the end of the week each bean was worth a penny.

I was in the middle of the first three children. My older brother either never did anything wrong or else he was smart enough not to get caught. My younger brother never really rocked the boat. With no competition, my transgressions were bold and bare. By Thursday, I usually had no beans left, and on Sunday when the accounts were settled, all I got was four new beans for the next week. I explained this system to Pete once and asked if he thought it would work with our kids.

"I doubt if a penny a bean would go over very well—with their new math they'd probably figure out how to subtract something from nothing."

That was when we had little problems; now we had big ones. We were learning about "acting out", "positive strokes", and "put-downs"; being a parent was becoming a difficult task. We had been through family counseling and lectures on improving family communications, but it seemed that the theory and the practice were hard to coalesce.

It was like Peter and the dike in the Dutch fable. We'd just get one of the children who had shot a BB gun at a car window straightened around when another one would be stopped by the police for careless driving. Shortly after I took each of our boys out to take his driver's test, I'd have to take a trip down to the traffic court for a speeding ticket. When I resented the time I had to spend with these summons, Pete reminded me that they probably inherited their heavy foot from me!

"Can't you learn from your brothers?" I asked Joe, as he took his turn. We were sitting in the waiting room of the judge's chambers. I had been to the same traffic court several times and could almost give the lecture myself . . . "It happens. You're trying to hurry home from work, or trying to make it home in time for your curfew. I can understand it happening once . . . the second time you come into this court, we have no mercy . . ." etc.

About this same time, as I was looking for some boards in our garage, I found some "funny green stuff" in the rafters. I reacted like most other post-WWII suburban mothers. I didn't know for sure what it was, but I had a good hunch. When I noticed a bunch of boys, including a couple of my own, hanging around the garage, I decided to question them. "Hey, you guys," I was trying to play it cool, "what's with this grass I found in the garage?"

"Huh? Grass? What'ya mean?" They responded almost in unison.

"Grass—pot—marijuana—you know very well what I mean. Where did it come from?"

"I dunno," my sons claimed innocently. Their friends were just as noncommittal.

"I guess I'll have to report it to the police," I threatened.

"Naw, Mom, why don't you just burn it up," one of my sons suggested. "I know where it came from. We were just horsing around with it. Don't worry, Mom, we're not into this stuff."

As each leak in the dike was plugged up with warnings, admonitions, and counseling, another hole would come uncorked. During these years we learned to grab the happy moments and enjoy them. We had ten years of Scouting, Little League, playing in the Assumption Band, class reunions, birthdays, and wedding anniversaries. In spite of their bickering, our kids still enjoyed doing things together. Even our illnesses and broken bones brought our family a little closer.

Chapter XXIV

When Pete's folks celebrated their golden wedding anniversary in 1967, we decided that we would make the supreme effort to atone for all the years of togetherness they had missed because we lived so far away. They had been doting grandparents, but mostly by long distance. Usually we took two or three of the children with us on our trips, but this time we would take all nine of them to Washington, D.C. We rationalized that it was better to go while both grandparents were healthy enough to enjoy us. Grandpa McKenna had already suffered a stroke and a heart attack.

But how do you transport eleven people from Minneapolis to Washington economically, safely, and sanely? Pete couldn't take time off to travel by car, and air fare for all of us was impossible. We compromised. I volunteered, "I guess the most logical way to go would be for you to fly out for the weekend, and I'll drive with the kids, huh? We could take our time."

Pete wasn't sure. "Do you think you could handle it alone? That's a lot of driving with nine kids in the car."

"It's no worse than driving to Browerville with them ten times!"

"But in three days?"

It was so simple—I wondered why people raised their eyebrows when we told them our plans.

It was an adventure from the time the six-year-old threw up on the other side of St. Paul until they removed me bodily from the car two and a half days later in Washington. When we stopped at a motel for the night I asked for their largest room, always ignoring their question, "How many in your party, ma'am?"

I tried for a room at the rear, "Could we have a room away from the lights and traffic, please?" I didn't want them to see how many of us emerged from the station wagon. The children insisted that we get a motel with a swimming pool, or as they called it, the family bath tub. As I sat trying to relax by the pool, one son popped out of the water, "Hey, Mom, watch me dive!"

"Be careful!" was all I could manage before he made a belly flop into the water.

"Mom, look at me swim!" six-year-old Paul yelled as he crawled in the shallow water.

"Mother, why don't you come in for a swim?"

"Hey, Mom, watch this!"

I could feel the eyes of the other pool-side travelers on me as they wondered, "How many of those kids belong to her, anyway?" They all did! I tried to shush my brood, then ignore them. Finally, I fled to the room. We separated the mattresses and box springs and used the chair cushions so that the ten of us were sacked out on wall-to-wall bed. Usually someone had to hopscotch over all of us to use the bathroom after we got settled for the night. The next morning we scurried to put the room back together and have our breakfast of dry cereal, juice, and tap water coffee. Other than periodically filling up the gas tank and emptying out the kids, which coincided if we were lucky, we were on the road until it was time for a picnic lunch. Once we stopped for a round of milk shakes to the tune of six dollars and fifty cents. We splurged for dinner in the evening, McDonald's Jumbo hamburgers. This was when they were into their "first million" and thirty cents bought you a lot of meat.

We played auto bingo, alphabet games, found forty-two states' license plates, sang "Ninety-nine bottles of beer on the wall," and in general, kept ourselves quite amused until the other side of Pennsylvania. Then map reading became a bore, and our ten passenger wagon seemed more like a VW "Bug." The family that travels together, fights together. I took a wrong turn into West

Virginia which put us on a detour. Nerves were wearing a little thin and by the time we got on the right road in Maryland, I rolled up the map and used it on whomever I could reach in the back seat.

The grandparents really must have loved us to welcome the mess we were when we arrived. They let me sneak off to bed while they got reacquainted with their grandchildren over grilled cheese sandwiches and chocolate milk shakes.

By the time Pete stepped off the plane, relaxed and refreshed after a two hour flight, we had all recovered from our hectic twelve hundred mile ride. He couldn't understand why I insisted that he take the youngest two children back with him on the plane.

This was to be the last time some of the children would see Pete's parents alive.

Chapter XXV

It seemed that whenever we thought we had the world by the tail and everything was going smoothly, we would be brought up short. We began to realize that when you have a large family, or even a small one for that matter, you have to be ready for any predicament, however shattering it may be.

I believe the most agonizing of our family's adversities occurred when our eighteen-year-old daughter confided to us that she was pregnant.

Pete exploded. I cried. This cannot be happening to us, I thought—and then instantly and foolishly—what will my mother say?

"How could you do this to us?" I yelled.

We were ill-prepared for anything like this, and we handled it clumsily. I thought it was the end of the world. Instead of being concerned about the turmoil and pain our daughter was suffering, I was worried about what people would think. How could I tell my friends? Where had we gone wrong?

I remember being consoled by the words of an understanding nun, "The good girls get pregnant; the sophisticated ones are on the pill or have abortions!" Our good friends, especially those who had suffered through a similar experience, gave us much needed support. Finally, my two brothers, one a priest and the other a psychiatric social worker, sat down with us and the unborn baby's father and his parents to discuss the situation calmly.

My brothers suggested several options to the young couple. "You don't have to feel that this is any reason to get married. In fact," Father Dick warned, "it's a very poor reason." We agreed on that.

He went on, "You can give the baby up for adoption if you feel that you're not ready for such a big responsibility. Or you can keep the baby and, if you still want to get married in a year or two, you'll be able to provide a stable home for it. The other route is to get married in the next month or two. I'd like to talk to each of you privately about this."

It seemed like an eternity. We four parents waited, visited nervously, and prayed during the counseling session. Finally, their son and our daughter returned to us—holding hands and smiling. Then the father-to-be announced, "We want our baby to be born into a family—ours, and we love each other enough to make any sacrifices to do this. We'd like your blessing on our marriage." Through all our tears, they were blessed. They were married by Father Dick, surrounded with loving support from their families and friends.

It has been a good marriage, and they both have assumed the responsibility that was thrust upon them at such an early age. They have worked together to establish their family, continue their education, and buy a home.

After my awkward handling of my daughter's pregnancy, I became a Birthright volunteer. This organization helps girls with counseling, encouragement, financial aid, or whatever they need to bring the child to term. I learned that you don't react with shock or rash judgment, and I have developed an empathy for not only the girl, but also for her parents.

Our first grandchild is very special to us. She was part of God's plan for our family to grow not only in size, but also in understanding.

Chapter XXVI

Pete had gone camping with the Boy Scouts since Jim was a Tenderfoot. He camped in tents when it was twenty degrees below zero and earned the Order of the Arrow award during one of their calling out ceremonies.

But Scouting isn't for everyone! We didn't realize this until one of our sons dutifully followed his brothers into Cubs, Webelows, and Tenderfoot. They had all raved about primitive camping and summer camp so we urged him, "Go and enjoy yourself. It'll make you rough and tough!"

His first postcard was written the day after he arrived: "This is terrible! I found six wood ticks on me today, the food is rotten, there's flies all over the place, and at night it freezes. I'm not having any fun, and I'm definitely not getting any relaxation. But I sure am getting rough and tough. Your dying son. . . ."

The next day he wrote: "I can't live like this for 2 weeks. Would you come and pick me up?"

The third day: "I'm still not having any fun. It rained all day today. I haven't gone to the bathroom in 3 days. I must be sick, so you better come and get me."

Later the third day: "You don't believe how lonely a guy gets way out here in the sticks. The 26th is family day and all the parents are coming. Would you come and pick me up? I'll still be rough and tough and you won't have to pay as much. It only takes two hours to get here by car. I'll never bug you again."

His last postcard: "I got your letter yesterday. I'm in activities, but they aren't any fun. Please drive up when you get this card, and bring me home. I'm really homesick. Besides one week of camp is long enough. We went on a 5-mile hike yesterday. I got second class and my first scalp. I love you and miss you and I'll see you Sunday."

When we drove into the campsite our boy scout was sitting on his duffle bag, all packed to go. One week was long enough for him, and we agreed.

Some women would buy a new hat to get out of the doldrums. I would make plans for remodeling or redecorating the house. When we moved to Oak Grove Boulevard, the house had three bedrooms, a den, a living room, a small kitchen and dining area, a basement room and an attached garage. We converted the den and basement to bedrooms immediately. The eleven of us shared the living room for two years. It was crowded; we watched TV, did homework, ironed, Pete read his Talking Book, and everyone had a friend over. Then we decided it was silly to give our car as much room as we had. We knocked out the garage wall and converted it to a family room. It was like raising the lid on a pressure cooker—we could spread out.

This remodeling was the beginning of a ten-year plan. We shared Dwight Eisenhower's feeling that he always wanted to leave a piece of property in better shape than he found it. Each year we've made some improvements—a new garage, driveway, patio, aluminum siding, roofing, carpeting and new wallpaper, closing in and winterizing the porch. Every time we approached the new project with very little knowledge. We knew nothing about cement, siding, roofing, insulation, or building in general. Pete's father and my grandfather were carpenters, but about all we inherited was the love of the smell of new wood. We learned though. By having three or four estimates for a particular project, we'd pick up tips on the right and wrong ways to have the job done.

It's too bad that once we were knowledgeable about these trades, we couldn't use them again. I don't think we'll ever re-roof in my lifetime! We always seemed to be repaying small loans, but our philosophy was, "Every year we wait, the price goes higher."

In my pre-marriage dream world, I had envisioned getting married, having children, sending them off to college, giving fabulous weddings. With old age would come grandchildren. My grandparents were old when I knew them, and I thought all grandparents were old. When I calculated the dates, they were all in their sixties because of late marriages. Gail Sheehy in *Passages* says, "With some mixture of heartache and relief, she (a mother) will watch that last babe board the school bus when she is 35."

That was not the case with me, however. When you have your last baby at thirty-eight and a half, there is no time between stages. When Jim was starting college, Paul was in the second grade. For eighteen years, we had children in Assumption Grade School. At the same time we had children in college, in the service, and married. It all blurs together. One advantage for me is that middle age lasts forever!

Chapter XXVII

Reviewing 1970 made my head swim. It started off with a bang—literally, on Nellie's tenth birthday in January. We were on our way to a sleigh ride with ten little girls in the back of our station wagon singing, "Dashing through the snow, in a one-horse open sleigh." As I entered a busy intersection that had a double set of traffic lights, a car started through the first light on amber and finished his way on red. We barely collided, but the impact swung our station wagon around and into a snow bank. The singing turned to squeals and shouts, "EEK!" "My gosh!" "Zowie." I turned around to see if any of the girls were hurt, and as they unscrambled themselves from the heap they were shaken, but smiling. "Are we stuck, Mrs. McKenna?"

I crawled out of my seat slowly to look—we were stuck! One back wheel was hanging over a ditch and the other was buried in icy snow. The other car had only a small dent in the side, and the driver volunteered to call a tow truck and my daughter. I didn't want to leave the girls alone in the station wagon, and I certainly didn't want all ten of them out on the road. We sang some more until the tow truck came to pull our car out; then Margaret piled all of us into her car and we went on to the sleigh ride. That was one of Nellie's more memorable birthdays.

In April, when Pete's father had another stroke, his mother called their doctor to the house. She had been taking care of Pop for the last year and it was difficult for her to leave him alone. While the doctor was there, she took him aside, and in her proper Boston modesty whispered, "Doctor, I've had this lump in my breast for a few months, and it seems to be getting larger." He had to ask to see it. After he felt it, he said, "You're both going to the hospital. Get your things together."

They operated two days later—a radical mastectomy. Pete's brother, Joe, agonized over the decision to have surgery. Without it, the doctor gave her a year to live. When Pete and I flew out to see them in the hospital, they were both progressing fairly well. We took his mother up to his father's room before they moved him to the Extended Care Unit. It was a heart-rending scene. Grandma McKenna was so used to watching over Pop that she felt she was shirking her duty by "putting him away." She kissed him, she patted him, and she reassured him that as soon as she was able, he could come back home with her.

A week later he had another stroke and died. Gram McKenna was still in the hospital, but she came home for the funeral. Pete and I flew out again. We were happy that all our children had come to their grandparents' golden wedding anniversary. We felt that was more important than attending his funeral.

Through the summer Gram had cobalt treatments and was quite miserable physically as well as emotionally. She missed Pop. They had been inseparable for over fifty-two years, and she felt she had no more purpose in her life. Our daughter, Margaret, went out to spend a month with her, but "Gram was not the same," she told us. For years she had talked incessantly about her grandchildren and showed their pictures to every one of her school cafeteria employees. When we met some of them at their anniversary open house, they knew each of her grandchildrens' names and something special about them. Now she didn't care if they were around or not. This made us sad. It was difficult to minister by long distance.

In August 1970, my own folks celebrated their golden wedding anniversary. It was the first time my brothers and sister and their families had all been together in sixteen years. There were twenty grandchildren and two great-grandchildren. Relatives and friends came from both coasts and many states in between. My mother and father had begun the plans for this day in early spring. They used the same system they used for my wedding in 1949—an exchange of labor with the same friends. Even the menu was similar with the Polish sausage and coffee cakes.

The weather was ideal (another answer to prayers), so that over four hundred people could come to the reception.

The Anniversary Mass, written and arranged by my brother Ted and his wife, was a family affair. My brother, Father Dick, was the celebrant, and my other brothers did the readings. Mother's sister, Aunt Rosie, played the organ, and cousin Marlene Williams sang two solos, combining a bit of the old church with the new. She sang "Ave Maria" in Latin, and as the jubilarians gave us their blessing she sang, "Like Olive Branches." Granddaughters read the petitions for blessings upon their grandparents, parents, grandchildren, great-grandchildren, and friends. Four grandsons were altar boys, two were ushers, and the small grandchildren presented their grandparents with spiritual bouquets. It was a time to remember, and everyone regretted that it couldn't last more than one day.

I had quit nursing several years ago, rather than work weekends. I had quipped that if ever I were offered a job on Tuesdays and Wednesdays from eight to three, I'd go back to work. I never thought it would happen, but now General Hospital, my old Alma Mater, had openings on Wednesdays and Thursdays from nine to three. I couldn't quibble over which days of the week. I was a medication assistant and all day I "passed meds." I felt like Scrooge in "Christmas Past" being back at General after twenty-three years. A new generation of student nurses rushed out the same door of the nurses' residence to classes at the University. A bus picked them up, but I remember we walked over to the campus to save the fifteen cents for something more essential—probably cigarettes, when we could get them.

On November 11, as we sat around the nurses' desk, I mentioned the "Big Blizzard" of 1940. No one, not even the interns, had even been born yet! To add to my self-image as an old fossil, it turned out that an intern's mother had been in nurses' training with me. I enjoyed being back at General, but by the end of each working day, I was exhausted by the awesome responsibility of giving out medications in a twenty bed ward. In Minneapolis, you could have three Andersons, two Johnsons, a Lindgren, a Lindstrom, and a Lundgren all in a row. They were supposed to have name bands on to be checked before being given their medications, but sometimes they took them off. When they sat up in a chair, it wasn't necessarily next to their own bed, so you couldn't go by the name on the bed either. And then some of them didn't know who they were when you asked them. After working for three years, I decided the stress wasn't worth the three and a quarter per hour I was being paid. I still had seven children at home, but our financial needs were being met.

In November of 1970 our sixteen-year-old daughter, Mary Catherine, had a spinal fusion to correct a congenital defect that was causing pain and numbness. They grafted a bone from her hip to make the fusion. The back surgery was successful, but she was unable to breathe into the "blow bottle" as she should have. When she developed pneumonia the doctors prescribed penicillin and within hours she broke out in a rash, her face swelled up and she had more difficulty breathing. She'd had penicillin before, but this time she had an allergic reaction to it. One more complication, the swelling under the cast, left her depressed, but all her brothers and sisters showered her with visits, calls, funny cards and gifts. After a month in the hospital she came home for Christmas and was able to go back to school in January wearing her plaster jacket.

By December, Pete's mother was complaining of a great deal of pain in her head and neck. We wanted her to come to Minnesota and spend Christmas with us, but she didn't feel up to it. "Please come, Mom," Pete pleaded. "We'll send you a plane ticket instead of buying any gifts." "Thanks, son, I'd come in a minute if I felt good. I'm afraid to be that far away from my doctor." We knew she meant it. We decided we'd surprise her and drive to Washington the day after Christmas, but our plans were pushed ahead a day when Pete's brother called to tell us she was in the hospital, for the cancer had spread. We were almost packed, so we left in the afternoon on Christmas Day with five of the children. We drove to Elgin, Illinois, the first night. We arrived at the hospital at eleven the next night, after driving the remaining seven hundred miles. We were a travel-weary mess, but all seven of us went directly to Gram's bedside. We were too late; she was in a coma. We spoke to her and squeezed her hand. Pete put his head close to her ear and shouted, "Mom, it's Pete!" but there was no response. This was hard for him to accept—he needed to hear her, to know she was still alive.

Each day we sat at the hospital hoping and praying she'd regain consciousness, but her doctor gave us little hope. He said she could die quickly or linger for months. We were staying in her house and nothing seemed right without her and Pop there. On the day before New Year's Eve we heard a big snowstorm was coming and the weather bureau told us if we left early in the morning, we could get to Pennsylvania and avoid it. That night we stood by my mother-in-law's bed and said goodbye. It was more like an ultimatum. I told her we had to go back to Minnesota and couldn't wait any longer. An hour after we left the hospital, she died.

It was difficult to let her go—our children had so many good memories of her as a fun-loving grandmother. She was a born entertainer and she told them stories that were nightmarish, but so full of exaggeration that they knew it was "make believe." We reminisced about the good times while we waited for the snowstorm to subside. Sixteen inches of snow crippled Washington, Virginia and Maryland. Thank goodness we hadn't left for Minnesota because I don't think they could have found us in time for the funeral.

We hadn't packed clothing that would be appropriate for the funeral, so I went to Montgomery Ward's with my credit card and picked up shirts and ties for the boys and new hose for the girls.

The wake was sad. We met a few of the old family friends and some of her employees, but the weather was so treacherous not many ventured out. As we sat waiting for the older generation to come and take over, I finally said to Pete, "You know what? This is it. We are the older generation." I realized what Emily Dickinson meant when she said, "Hold your parents tenderly, for your world will never be the same after they're gone."

The trip home was a nightmare of rain, sleet, fog and snow in the mountains, and more ice through Chicago and Wisconsin. We had started 1970 off on ice and ended it the same way.

It was hard to accept the deaths of Pete's parents. A year before they were living a full life—her first year of retirement. We had often assessed our children's good fortune to have both sets of grandparents for so many years. We speculated who would "go first" and who would best be able to handle the loss. But we never really thought it would happen *yet*. It was several years before I fully realized I couldn't send pictures and letters telling them about their grandchildren anymore.

Chapter XXVIII

It was a new year, 1971, and life must go on. We resumed our jobs, our winter fun, and our school activities. When I was forty, I decided I would learn to swim. No one should live among 10,000 lakes and not know how to swim. Before I was fifty, I was determined to learn to ski. I had skated all my life, but to really enjoy Minnesota winters, skiing was the "in" thing. I learned downhill first, and although I never progressed to more than the medium slopes, it is a thrill to career down the hills with the wind biting your face. With the cap, the goggles, the ski outfit and the boots covering me from head to toe, all age barriers are gone—no one knew if that five foot daredevil was fifteen or fifty. Skiing was such fun I thought Pete should enjoy it too. We rented cross-country skis and glided across the flat snow-covered lake. It wasn't as exhilarating as downhill, but we kept at it and bought cross-country skis of our own. It's difficult for Pete to get a good grip on the pole with the three fingers of his left hand, but he's able to stay on the trails by following me. His understatement of the winter was, "I like it better than skating—"

One evening at the end of March as I was coming out of the confessional at church, a friend grabbed my arm and whispered, "There's a telephone call for you at the rectory."

A hundred thoughts crossed my mind. Pete? An accident? I remembered the same feeling when we'd been paged at a restaurant or dance, and all our kids wanted to know was if they could drink the pop in the refrigerator.

112

I hurried to the rectory, and shakily picked up the receiver. It was Mary Catherine. "Now, Mom, don't get excited. There's been an accident—Paul was hit by a car—but not bad. The ambulance is on the way."

I drove home in a frenzy and as I approached the corner, I saw the flashing lights of the police cars and ambulance. I jumped out of my car and ran across the street. Three of my children grabbed me and led me to the ambulance. As the police lifted the litter, Paul raised his head and smiled. "Hi, Mom, it's just my arm," he chirped. What a relief!

As I followed the ambulance to the hospital, my mind wandered back a few years to the day when my son had come running in to tell me a little girl had been hit by a car on this same corner. She was Colleen O'Hara, a beautiful six-year-old who had moved to the neighborhood only a few weeks earlier. When I had seen her lying in the street, I didn't think she was alive, so I had gone in to be with her mother. I had met the mother, Eileen O'Hara, only once before, but Colleen and Nellie had become good friends. When I had come in to tell her about the accident, Eileen had been painting a bedroom. I had helped her get down from the ladder, and had hoped by the time we got out to the street the ambulance would be there. It was. They were lifting the child's battered body into the back door of the van, her head swathed in bandages.

I remembered that after the ambulance had driven off, my new friend, Eileen O'Hara, and I had driven to the hospital. We both had dreaded going in. Colleen was alive, but her life hung by a fragile thread. She'd had a skull fracture and was in a coma. Her poor mother had been frantic—her husband, Ed, had been in flight somewhere on a business trip, she didn't know a doctor, much less a neurosurgeon, and hadn't registered in a parish to call a chaplain. With my early experience in the Emergency Room, I'd been able to help her with these decisions. The rest of the time we had prayed. Three weeks had gone by before Colleen opened her eyes, and the first person she had called was "Nellie." We thought it had been a miracle. I had asked my friend, Father Kelly, to pray for her, and the day he had called to tell me that he had offered his mass for her, she'd regained consciousness. Our families became close, and although the O'Haras have moved out of our neighborhood, they have not moved out of our lives. "Sweet are the uses of adversity."

Now I was waiting in the examining room for the doctor's diagnosis on my own son. "It's just my arm" became a compound, comminuted fracture—his elbow was smashed to pieces. We called our orthopedic surgeon, Dr. McMahon, and he worked for three hours to clean out the wound and lay the pieces in place. He "pinned" the elbow and put it in traction at a right angle. Several weeks later after the wound healed, he put it in a cast. Paul was in the hospital for one month, and someone from our family visited him everyday. On Easter Sunday we all went in after mass with his Easter bunny, which was bright pink and three feet tall. He learned to write with his left hand so he could keep up with his school work. His teacher, Sister Herman Joseph, was very helpful with assignments, and his classmates entertained him with cards, letters and gifts. He still has a cross made from chips of glass that his friend Dave gave him.

To make our life even more hectic, one of the weeks Peter III was in the hospital, Paul was in the next room, with a kidney infection!

That summer in June, when my brother, Father Dick, celebrated his silver jubilee as a Crosier priest, he had three parties. For the formal one in Browerville, my brothers and sister and their families came from Maryland, New York and Wisconsin for another reunion. Father Dick was the Provincial of the Crosier order in the United States at that time, an office comparable to that of a bishop of a diocese. He left home to go to the seminary when he was fourteen years old, but he has always stayed close to his family. When my sister, Jackie, and I had sixteen youngsters between us, he visited our homes whenever he needed to strengthen his vocation.

After our week at the lake with our friends, the Andersens, seven summers ago, we had decided that our families should share more good times. We added other families and went canoeing down the St. Croix River. It was a learning experience for most of us—you couldn't "paddle your own canoe", for it was teamwork. We had left the makings for a picnic at our destination, eighteen miles down river. That was wise, for the kids worked up such an appetite paddling that the food would've been gone before we reached the picnic grounds. In the winter we pooled our resources and kids for a sleigh ride party. The object of the game seemed to be shoving the mothers and fathers off the sleigh. We ran behind in the tracks and once in a while the driver would stop to retrieve us breathless oldsters. The generation gap faded like our frosty breath. The hot chocolate and hot dogs afterwards helped us thaw out. During one summer we gathered twenty-eight for a bike hike. We drove vans and cars out to a little traveled road around a lake and then got on our bicycles. Pete and I had our tandem; some had toddler seats or baskets with their youngsters tied in. Again, our day ended with a big picnic in a friend's yard—she had a cottage on the lake.

We had summer, fall, and winter outings with our families, and when the children started asking, "What are we going to do for spring?", we surprised them. One Sunday in early March we packed our picnic lunch, charcoal, hot dogs and all, and drove over to Minnehaha Park. We brushed the snow from the tables and fire pots and set out our picnic. We had the whole park to ourselves.

Chapter XXIX

For over ten years Pete had been camping in tents, or on tarps under the stars. He loved to get away in the woods or near a lake with other men or our boys. His nirvana was sitting around the bonfire trading stories about "WWII" or telling his sons stories of the early west. After his mother died he got a check from her retirement fund and we all felt that Gram's legacy should be a pop-up tent camper. We even christened it "Flossie" in her honor.

Pete immediately began planning a two week camping trip with his boys. He called Yellowstone National Park to reserve a campsite at Fishing Bridge. Then he had John, Peter and his friend, Bob, study maps and plan the route. The boys were 18, 13 and 12.

When the four of them left at five o'clock in the morning we were all there with cameras, advice and goodbye kisses. The station wagon, with John at the wheel, was jammed with food and equipment. Although I was apprehensive about the trip I was glad John was driving instead of me. Camping was not my favorite way to travel. Our camper had all the comforts of modern outdoor living—but cooking, eating, dressing, sleeping and house-keeping in eight-by-ten-foot space was not my idea of a vacation.

The trip was exciting for the boys because they had never been west before. The first night they camped on the Missouri River and saved some of the muddy water to bring home to me. When they stopped at the famous Wall Drug Store the next day for "free ice water," they met our neighbors, returning from their trip west, who brought us a first hand report about our travelers.

By the time they reached Yellowstone the boys were enthralled by the mountains. Fishing Bridge Campgrounds, however, was a disappointment . . . just a slab of cement without shade. Fishing from there was even more disappointing—the anglers stood ten deep trying to get their hooks into the stream. Pete and the boys decided they'd do other things. Each morning they packed a lunch and drove through a different area of the park. One day they followed a guide to the top of a mountain and went sliding in the snow. That was a treat for Minnesotans in July.

After several days at Yellowstone they decided to move on to the Tetons. "More scenery," Pete said ironically, as he related the trip to me, "you know that's my favorite pastime."

On their way back through Billings they blew a hole in the muffler, but John patched it up with a pop can. "That was our only car trouble," Pete reported, but back in Minnesota at a campgrounds in Detroit Lakes they had another scare. John was out on the lake fishing, unaware of a tornado warning. Pete and the boys tried to signal him, but eventually they had to go inside as the tornado approached. If they hadn't folded up the tent camper it would have been blown away, Pete told me later.

When the winds subsided Pete and the owner of the lodge went down to the lake, both fearing the worst for John. All his boats were up on shore and turned upside down. "Well, I'll be darned—how—I sure thought—gee I wonder—I sure thought I'd lost all these boats." He shook his head unbelievingly and started to turn them right side up. There was John, asleep under one of them. He was exhausted from his rescue work!

Pete summed up the experience, "A camper that sleeps seven is fine if all seven are sleeping, but three teenage boys are a crowd, especially on a rainy day!"

My parents were married for over fifty years and they were still thrilled each time they had another grandchild. Two of my brothers and their wives blessed them in 1971. James and Peggy had a baby boy—a namesake and as people threw the cliche at them, "a comfort in their old age."

"Like right now," retorted my brother, who was forty-three.

My "baby" brother, Ted, and his wife, Mary, adopted a son, Brian David, the first black grandchild. The grandparents were asked by the social service agency how they felt about the adoption and they responded with love. They flew to Milwaukee for the christening.

They were also being blessed with great grandchildren. "May you see your children's children even to the third and fourth generation" (Tobias 9:9-11). Our daughter and her husband had another baby girl. Once again our whole family's cup runneth over.

Our joys always seemed to balance the hectic side of our family life. We still had six children at home; three in high school. They had jobs and had to share one car to get to work. Arranging schedules and rides so that no one ended up a pedestrian (Heaven forbid!) was quite a logistics feat. They all worked in eating establishments which helped shrink our grocery bill somewhat. I guess we were lucky they were working. The high school kids were still suffering the fallout from the rebellion and defiance of the sixties, some of it justified, against the establishment. Hair was long and unkempt, clothes were faded and wrinkled, and even their attitude was negative; school did not "turn them on." We had to keep hoping and praying that "this, too, shall pass."

At times it seems that Pete and I led a charmed life. We were at the right place at the right time. One Saturday evening in October, my cousin's husband called to ask if we were busy that night.

"We're always busy, Jim. What do you have in mind?" I asked flippantly. They had a larger family than ours so I thought it was just a rhetorical question. He knew the answer.

"Could you and Pete be ready in half an hour and I'll pick you up and take you to the St. Paul river landing? We have . . . "

"Slow down, Jim. Where to? What?"

"Joni and I have reservations on the *Delta Queen* river boat, but we can't get away tonight. I thought maybe you and Pete could ride down the river tonight, and we'll meet you in Winona tomorrow. Then you can drive our car back to Minneapolis and we'll ride the boat back. . . . You have to say yes or no right now."

I held onto the phone as I explained the plan hurriedly to Pete. Without hesitating he said, "Say yes!"

Our daughter, Margaret, was home from college for the weekend so babysitting was no problem. We packed our toothbrushes and Jim raced us to the boat.

What unexpected elegance! We had never heard of the *Delta Queen,* much less ever expected to ride on it. We had the most expensive stateroom on the top deck, but we didn't realize the luxury of it until we peeked into the tiny cubicles on the lower decks. The Captain welcomed us to the dining room and we joined another couple who was sitting alone. After the initial introductions we learned that Pete and our new friend were in the same battalion of the 80th Infantry Division and were fighting at the same time and place in Europe. That, in itself, made the night for Pete. A stage show, a sing-a-long and "ice breakers" made it one grand party.

The next morning we had a continental breakfast. Later, as we sat on the deck and feasted our eyes on the beauty of October's panorama of colors along the banks of the Mississippi River, I wished that like an artist chooses colors, I could choose words to describe the scene to Pete.

When we docked at Winona about noon, a chaplain came aboard and offered mass for those who wished to attend.

About three o'clock Jim and Joni arrived to board for the return trip to St. Paul. How do you thank people for a memorable time? We couldn't. We just drove off in their Cadillac, still feeling like Cinderella and the Prince. We knew midnight would come quickly when we got back home!

Chapter XXX

The drums go bang, the cymbals clang
The horns, they blaze away. . . .
And Hennessey tutelly toots the flute
And the music is somethin' grand.

South Boston? New York's Fifth Avenue? No, it's St. Patrick's Day in Minneapolis. The Grand Marshal could be Mort Sahl or Hubert Humphrey, the tenor singing "Danny Boy" could be the Norwegian mayor, and the music could be the Polish polka band from "Nordeast" Minneapolis. There are a few genuine Irish bands from Waverly and Green Isle, but mostly we have to settle for leftovers from St. Paul, the original Irish ghetto. Across the river they have thousands of Irish families in various shades of green marching, singing and drinking. They finally had to outlaw motorized vehicles and liquor. In Minneapolis where we Irish are outnumbered by Scandinavians we have only hundreds of families, not even all Irish, but the enthusiasm is just as spirited.

My friend, Lois Patricia Hennessey Andersen, was born on St. Patrick's Day, and we don't let her forget it from the time we go to mass in the morning until we fold ranks at the Knights of Columbus Hall after midnight.

One St. Patrick's Day seemed more memorable because our friends, the O'Haras, came up from Omaha to join in the "annual celebration." They thought they had over-imbibed when they met

120

St. Patrick on Nicollet Avenue—green mitre, gold staff, and all. That evening we thrilled to Pat O'Brien's song and wit at Diamond Jim's Supper Club. When we visited Pat in his dressing room, we were amazed at his pep and sparkle; almost like his Father Duffy and Knute Rockne days on the screen.

Our children were excused from school "for cultural study" and we all met at "our corner" on 10th and Marquette Avenue. Aunts, uncles, cousins, in-laws who weren't Irish, anyone who wanted to march behind the HOY-DUFFY banner joined our clan.

This particular year we had temperatures in the fifties, but our costumes varied with the weather. Minnesota can have blizzards or balmy days in March, and we have bundled up in fur coats and caps or stripped down to an Irish sweater and paper derby.

After most of the parade had passed by, we stepped into place and marched with them. We usually had to step warily, as horses had preceded us. The people lining the streets gave us a tolerant smile; they didn't seem to understand how we could be having so much fun.

At the end of the parade we met at a plaza on the Nicollet Mall for a sing-a-long, led by our Scandinavian mayor. After that, it was time for lunch. The grown-ups went to Murray's Bar and Restaurant for Irish stew and we sent the kids to McDonald's under the trusted guardianship of our son, Peter James III. We had barely settled in at Murray's with an Irish coffee, when we heard a tap on the window. Eleven kids had their noses pressed flat against the glass watching us. Peter's revenge for making him babysit.

Other years we've gone to Duff's Irish Pub, which is wall-to-wall Irishmen from morning till closing in the wee hours. A roving colleen will paint a green shamrock on your cheek for a price. They also serve a delicious Irish stew.

The youngsters enjoy going to the open house at the Dublin Walk, an Irish import shop. They have native dancers doing the jigs and reels, and everyone in the audience has his toes tapping. Their sales people, who have a delightful brogue, serve cake and coffee.

When Pete couldn't get away from his stand at the city hall, we all marched into the hallowed halls, waving our green balloons

and banners, singing McNamara's Band. He feigned embarrassment, but after we attracted half the police force, he would join us
in singing his favorite, "Harrigan."

I have often thought it would be a long-overdue gesture of
friendliness and cooperation if Minneapolis and St. Paul, the Twin
Cities, would each march to the bridge on the Mississippi River
and raise the Irish flag in the middle of it. The mayors, even
though Norwegian and Jewish, could exchange keys to their re-
spective cities, tied with a green bow, of course.

> *Until that time, we'll be loyal to Minneapolis*
> *'and though we're few in number*
> *We're the finest in the land!'*

Chapter XXXI

Where two or more of my family are gathered, there we go also, especially if the two are my brother, James, and his wife, Peggy. They have a knack for hospitality. Whether it's a one bedroom flat with six people squeezed in or a three story house—the door is always open. Each person is treated specially.

When James was asked to teach a summer session at Harvard University in 1972, the gears in Peggy's "Perle Mesta" mind started to grind. Why not rent a house on the beach and invite everyone to come? She did, and we did.

Once again, when we planned to travel for a couple of weeks, Pete didn't feel we could afford to hire a substitute at his stand for the whole time. I was beginning to get the idea; he didn't enjoy my kind of traveling. Again, he planned to fly to the east coast, join us for part of the trip, and then fly back home.

Margaret, Peter and I started off on the most interesting, spontaneous, fun trip we had ever taken. With two of us sharing the driving, we reached Fort Wayne, Indiana, the first night without much pushing. Father Dick had his own "Provincial's Quarters", and he cooked us a delicious steak dinner. This surprised us. He could fly a plane, print a newspaper, play the piano, snow and water ski, dance on roller skates, run the Crosier Order of priests, but he had never even tried cooking. It was a new challenge for him; of course, he didn't settle for hamburger hot dish specials like his sisters. He became a gourmet. Since then he has taken up furniture making.

The three of us stopped whenever and wherever we pleased—
scenic views, historic markers, antique shops—every place I had
wanted to stop but was afraid to ask when Pete was with us. In
earlier years we had visited Barbara Fritchie's house in Freder-
ick, Maryland. Now that I looked the part I wanted to stick my
head out the window and shout John Greenleaf Whittier's poem:

> *'Shoot if you must, this old gray head,*
> *But spare your country's flag', she said.*

Peter and Marg were indulgent. There would be things they
wanted to do, too.

We stopped at Woodbridge, Virginia, to visit my cousin, Bob
John, and his wife, Mickey. Bob's mother and father were divorced
when he was a young boy in Minneapolis, but his father brought
him to Browerville occasionally to visit our grandparents. Years
later when I was in training at General Hospital in Minneapolis
and Bob was in the service, we met again. His father was dying in
a nearby hospital, and I spent as much time as I could with Uncle
Robert. Bob and I corresponded for the "duration" and we kept
in touch when he went back to the University after the war. When
Pete and I lived in Washington, D.C., he came out there to find a
job, but when we moved back to Minnesota, we lost him. I
thought about him each time we were in Washington, but no one
knew where he was. One time I took all three telephone direc-
tories, Maryland, Virginia and the District of Columbia, and tried
every Robert John that was listed. He couldn't lose me like that!
After wrong numbers and "no one listed by that name", I finally
found him in Woodbridge, Virginia. It had been fifteen years since
we'd talked, and after an hour of catching up we promised to keep
in touch forever after. He had since been back to Minnesota for
my mother and father's golden wedding anniversary, and now we
returned the visit. They took us to nearby Dale City to watch the
Fourth of July fireworks, but unfortunately they were dampened
by the severe floods that year and lost most of their flare and
color.

Earlier this year we had gold aluminum siding and black shut-
ters put on our house—another legacy from Pete's folks' estate.

Our neighbor, who is originally from Boston, began to call our home "Williamsburg West." I wanted to see what Williamsburg East was like, so we went. We did what all the tourists did—locked each other in the stock and pillories, bought tri-cornered souvenir hats, and drank ale at Raleigh's Tavern. But we also were awed by the historic sanctity of Bruton Parish Church where early American patriots prayed for guidance in their struggle for freedom. In the capitol where Patrick Henry delivered his famous speech, I remembered the words, "Is life so dear or peace so sweet as to be purchased at the price of chains and slavery? Forbid it, Almighty God! I know not what course others may take, but as for me, give me liberty or give me death!" Margaret and Peter cringed as I recited the passage. I guess kids don't memorize any more.

Of all the craft shops where colonial arts and trades are demonstrated, I liked the Printer and Bookbinder the best. Spreading the word was vital in those early days, but the printing methods were laborious and slow. The bookbinder had to start with the basics—making the paper, the ink, the glue, and the dye for the colored fly leaves of the hand-sewn books.

When we drove back north to Washington after almost a week of traveling, we met Pete and our son, Joe, at the airport. Pete had a fifth of champagne bulging out of the pocket of his sport coat and he and Joe were enjoying some private joke. It seems United Airlines had some in-flight games for their passengers, like how many pounds of fuel would the plane use on its flight from Minneapolis to Washington? There were army colonels and seasoned traveling men on board, but Joe and Pete figured out the answer and won the bottle.

This was our first visit since Gram and Gramp McKenna died, and Washington was not the same. There was no focal point, no base of operations. We visited their graves near Catholic University, said a prayer, and cried. Living back in Minnesota, we hadn't been struck with reality yet.

Joe, Peter, and Margaret enjoyed touring the same places their grandparents had taken them on previous visits, but like going back home, nothing was as big or as exciting as it was when they held on to Grandma's hand and listened to her travelogue. We all enjoyed the new Kennedy Center and the new additions to the Smithsonian Institute. On our way north we stopped to enjoy the hospitality of another brother, Harry. He had given up any desire for automobile travel since our ill-fated honeymoon trip to California, so the only way we could visit with him was to go to Laurel, Maryland.

Joe and Peter wanted another adventure, a ride on the Metroliner from Washington to New York at one hundred and twenty miles an hour. They had their own money, so off they went. We met them in Staten Island at Bob Reilly's house. Bob was another of Pete's cousins we hadn't met since we were married. Bob, Kathy, and their daughter, Patty, were delightful hosts, and I was thrilled to meet a McKenna relative. Pete had only eight cousins, compared to my fifty-four, and we still hadn't met all of them.

The next morning as we were starting our drive into Manhattan to attend a show at Radio City and make a visit to St. Patrick's Cathedral, Kathy Reilly gave us this sage and down-to-earth advice: "New York gets awfully uncomfortable if you have to go to the toilet and can't find one. Just walk into the lobby of the Waldorf Astoria and use their facilities. You might as well use the best!"

In Pawtucket and Valley Falls, Rhode Island, Bob Reilly's brother, Joe, gave us a tour of the original McKenna family home. I was happy to see that Pete's great-grandfather's house had been restored and was still lived in. I think it's sad to see a neglected, obsolete house that has served its time as a family shelter and then been left in ruins because of death, taxes, right of way, or whatever.

Pete's father and uncle had started a cement block factory in Valley Falls after World War I and they were doing very well until they had to decide whether to "go big" to match the demand and competition. They couldn't get the capital to expand so eventually they abandoned the business. Joe Reilly showed us the site of the factory. He also took us to the cemetery where Pete's grandparents, aunts, and uncles are buried. Pete didn't remember ever being there before. We dug out the family headstone, cleaned it off, and stood it upright. A little cement from the factory would've helped!

The original purpose of this meandering trip was to visit James and Peggy at Rockport, Massachusetts. Peggy had found "Mr. Gray's Cabin"—a large, fully furnished house only two hundred yards from the shore. It was the kind of house that made you feel at home immediately. Books were there for your reading, games were set out for your playing, and Peggy always had the table set for the eating. She fit into this whole picture as though she had spent her whole life on the New England shore. But she had always been able to have a chameleon-like response: if she were talking to her sister Alice she used a Brooklyn accent, with her Irish mother she had the brogue, with her southern friends she drawled. I can imagine if she wanted to imitate her Minnesota in-laws she'd have a good midwestern twang.

To celebrate our arrival we were going to have a little toast, but James and Peggy hadn't been in Rockport long enough to find out the town was dry.

"Never fear," said Pete, as he sent Joe out to the car. He came back with the bottle of champagne they had won on the plane.

The quaint shops, the seafood, the shrimp boats, and Motif Number One were an artist's dream come true, but for us it was the atmosphere. The sea air and breeze was a tonic—each morning we took our thermos and cups to the shore and had coffee "on the rocks." As we sat and watched the waves splash up over the rocks and then recede into the ocean until another batch came up, we became mesmerized. The water seemed to wash away all the stress and frustrations that had accumulated for each of us. We were tranquilized and could have become addicted, but our time ran out. We had to get back into the hurry and bustle of the real world.

Pete and Joe took the plane from Boston to Minneapolis, and Peter, Marg and I got back on the road. We took the scenic route northwest from Rockport, up through the White Mountains of New Hampshire. As we got farther west into the Green Mountains of Vermont, I asked my navigator, "Where is Stowe, Vermont?" Peter found it on the map. "It's about twenty-two miles northeast of Montpelier. Why, what's in Stowe, Vermont?"

"Do you remember seeing *The Sound of Music* and reading *The Trapp Family Singers?*"

Both he and Margaret remembered. I had read the book aloud to the whole family, and we had seen the movie several times.

"How would you two like to stay at Maria Von Trapp's Lodge?"

They weren't as excited about the idea as I was, but on this trip we were all agreeable and ready for any new adventure.

It was late afternoon when we finally found the road out of Stowe and the steep climb to the Trapp Family Lodge. As we approached the place we felt as though we were in the Austrian Alps with Maria dancing through the meadow singing, "The hills are alive with the sound of music." The mountain view and the trees surrounding a quiet pool were breath-taking, but the lodge itself won our hearts. It looked like an Alpine chalet with three tiered balconies, each level covered with petunias, begonias, zinnias, and marigolds of every hue. When we arrived the baroness herself was out weeding the gardens. She didn't look a bit like Julie Andrews!

We thought the price for our two rooms was high until we sat down to a seven-course Austrian dinner which included wiener schnitzel, popovers, and warm apple strudel. Baroness Von Trapp visited with us at our table and posed for a picture. She was pleasant, but brusque and businesslike.

After dinner we hiked, or more aptly, scaled up to the family chapel. It was built at the top of a steep hill and we figured the only way they could have hauled the heavy stones up there was to do it in the winter and use a sled. There were fresh flowers and a vigil light burning at the altar. Above it was a picture of Mary, Our Lady of Peace.

Later in the evening we went into a cellar-like Austrian bar, the Tiroler Stueberl, and joined in the community sing. There was a professional director for the Schnitzelbank song.

Breakfast was five courses, still included in our bill for the night's lodging. We decided that some day we'd come back in the winter and go cross-country skiing to work up an appetite for all the delicious heavy food.

After two weeks of travel and living out of a suitcase I was anxious to get back home. Margaret and Peter felt the same way. We ferried across Lake Champlain to get into New York State, and then drove across on the thruway with as few stops as possible. At Niagara Falls we hurried over to the Canadian side and took a quick look at the lights reflected on the falls. It's a good thing it was dark because we wouldn't have waited! The next day we crossed Ontario and Michigan and put the car on the Chessie Line Ferry at Luddington. On our five hour ride to Manitowoc, Wisconsin, Marg and Peter had pooled their money and rented a berth for me to get some sleep. After all that driving I couldn't get into neutral very quickly, but I did manage a couple hours of sleep. When we debarked in Wisconsin we kept right on driving. It was six o'clock in the morning when we drove into our driveway at home. Pete was just leaving for work.

Chapter XXXII

Life wasn't all exciting trips, but when I look back at photograph books I don't see pictures of daily humdrum. We had the same routine as other families—laundry every other day, groceries to buy, meals to cook, housecleaning, and yard work. Every fall we had a family rake-off—as many as one hundred and twenty bags of oak leaves. In the last five years we've lost four huge trees with oak wilt so we feel lucky that we still have a dozen or more healthy trees dropping their leaves and acorns.

With Nellie and Paul still in Assumption School I was involved with driving players and cheerleaders to football games. This was a sacrifice for me because I could never understand why anyone would want to stand out in all kinds of weather to watch a bunch of boys knock each other around trying to get a ball away so they could run with it.

Peter and Joe were at Richfield High School and into speech contests, photography, and the nuts and bolts of cars in our driveway. We had a dark room in our basement; it was originally a closet for canned fruits and vegetables, but I had given up on gardening after we moved to this shady lot. The boys had taken film making as well as still photography and one day Joe and his friend staged and filmed a hold-up at the gas station where they worked. When the film was developed the boys borrowed a splicer and put their masterpiece together. As they sat in our dark basement and turned on the projector I heard a scream of horror and then laughter. The movie opened with somebody's grandparents arriving for Christmas Eve, the distribution of gifts, the delighted grandchildren showing off their toys and much, much more. With their assignment due in three days the mix-up by the photo company became less humorous, but the store manager wrote a note to their teacher explaining what had happened and gave them more film to re-stage their hold-up. They wished that they could do a sequel to their story; a shot of the other people watching what they thought were their Christmas pictures!

Besides the humdrum, we had birthday parties twice a month from January till May and we made each one special. When our children turned sixteen we took them out to dinner alone, wherever they wanted to eat. For the first six or so this was a big treat. As the older children moved away from home and McDonald's was selling its billionth hamburger, eating out became a more common occurrence. By the time Nellie reached sixteen she wanted to eat at Mr. Steak so that the whole family could be with her. Times change.

The next summer, in 1973, the Greyhound Bus Company offered a thirty day excursion rate for traveling any place in the United States for $149. Our son Peter III had been exposed to just enough of the country to whet his appetite for more. Although he was only fifteen and a half, he and his friend, Bob, worked to save enough money for the bus fare, food and lodging for a month. They went into the matchbook printing business with the stamping machine we had used in the Marian Shop years before. They went through the neighborhood soliciting business. Then with a small loan from his father, Peter invested in several thousand blank match books. They browsed over maps and schedules to plan a complete tour of the United States—starting from Minnesota across to Seattle, down through California, across to Texas, New Orleans, Florida, up the east coast to Washington, New York, and Boston, thence back across Ohio, Indiana, Illinois, Wisconsin, and home.

Before they left, both boys went through their parents' address books and wrote to relatives and friends around the country who might be willing to put them up for a day or two. They are still our friends so the boys must have left a good impression.

Twice we got calls from YMCAs asking if the boys had our permission to travel. I guess the west coast has a thousand runaway kids coming in every day.

Toward the end of their trip we planned to meet in South Bend, Indiana, at the bus depot. When Peter was asked later what was the best part of the whole trip, he answered, "Seeing my mother in South Bend." Being broke by that time may have been what prompted such deep feeling for me.

Several years before the Bicentennial and *Roots* started an upsurge in genealogy, my brothers and I had decided to write the history of our family and present it to our father on his eightieth birthday.

Fortunately, my brother Harry works for the Archives in Washington and he knew the process for finding immigration and boat arrival lists. He also travels a great deal and on one of his trips he spent a few days tracing our father's origins in Silesia back to 1793.

My mother's ancestors were born in Ireland and came over in the 1840's. There were no written records of their lives in Ireland because most of the church records were hidden or destroyed by fire, and the majority of the immigrants coming to the United States, especially the Catholic ones, were illiterate.

I visited the church in Belle Plaine, Minnesota, where my Irish ancestors had settled. Many of the stained-glass windows were donated by my relatives. I saw the original "Duffy farm", and the spot where my grandmother taught school. I copied the birth, marriage, and death records at the church and at the county court house. So many died of "quinsy", old age, or childbirth.

It was hard to believe that we knew so little about our own father and mother's background. Every time I could corner a relative I'd get out my notebook to record the date, a name, or an anecdote. I met relatives I never knew existed, and several of them said, "We should get together sometime other than at wakes and funerals." "OK," I came right back at them, "you notify everyone in your family that on the third Sunday in July we'll have a picnic at St. John's Church in Belle Plaine, right next to the cemetery that holds all our forefathers. Tell them to bring a picnic lunch to share."

They all came—about sixty of them, and cousins met cousins they hadn't seen in fifty years. They were all in the sixties, seventies, and eighties and they were happy to have their pictures taken together.

As I walked through the graveyard with some of them I gleaned more history of the family. My notebook was filling up with stories of who was an industrious farmer, who ran away to the Gold Rush, who drank too much, and who built the church. We dragged out all kinds of skeletons, but most of their ancestors were a source of pride to the family.

Another good fortune in putting our book together was that Father Dick knew something about printing and also knew the man in the Crosier Monastery at Onamia, Minnesota, who ran their press. I spent a couple of days there arranging pictures, setting pages in order, and proofreading. Early in November we had the finished product—a forty page history of the John-Hoy families.

On my father's eightieth birthday, November 23, we had an open house for him and presented him with a leather bound version of our book. With all his children, his grandchildren (which by now included two black Vietnamese children my brother, Ted, and his wife, Mary, had adopted), four great-grandchildren, and hundreds of relatives and friends present, we toasted a man who had spent his whole life working for the welfare of other people. Daddy was choked up and speechless.

Chapter XXXIII

Early in 1974, I realized that Pete and I would be celebrating our twenty-fifth wedding anniversary in June. I could hardly believe that it had been that long, but when I considered how full the years had been it seemed that we had always been married. We originally took each other for better or for worse, but now we just took each other for granted.

After twenty-five years, during which he had never seen me, I wondered if I had really seen him. No one had given me a course on how to live with a blind husband, and I have made many mistakes. Now that we were passing a milestone in our life, and our nine children no longer took up all my time, I thought I would like to study and understand what blindness is and what it does to a person, Pete in particular. How does he manage to go off to his vending stand every morning at six-thirty with only a white cane in his hand and a rosary in his pocket?

To start my study, I naively thought I would learn how it felt to be blind by spending twenty-four hours blindfolded. I knew being without sight for a day would help me understand the physical difficulties of blindness, but because I knew that tomorrow I would see again, I could not realize the psychological problems involved.

After Pete and the children left in the morning, I put blinders on my eyes. Right after I did that, I realized that I hadn't looked into the mirror to see what I looked like and had to guess that my hair and everything else was in shape. I didn't dare put my wig on because I didn't know whether I would put it on straight or not. I went out to the kitchen. I know how my husband guides himself with his one arm out ahead so that he doesn't bump into things.

I made my way to the coffee pot and never realized what a big production my ten cups of coffee a day would be. I heated it too hot so that I couldn't touch the spout to guide it into the cup, much less put my finger into the cup to see how full it was. I had to wait for my first cup of coffee. Then I poured myself a bowl of cereal and searched the kitchen for wherever the children left the sugar. When I sat down to eat, I didn't have any trouble finding my mouth, but I don't think that I would have liked to have been in a restaurant where anybody was watching me. The last part of the bowl, I just lifted to my lips and drank.

When I started to do the dishes, I found that the dishwasher was full and had to be emptied; but, before I could empty it, I had to be sure that the cupboard top was clear so that I could put things on it and know where they were. I made piles of each type of plate and saucer and got them all put away. Then I started on the dirty dishes. About that time the telephone rang and I grabbed the towel to wipe my hands, and went over to the phone to talk to a friend a few minutes—then I came back and I couldn't remember what I had been doing. I also wanted to wipe my hands again and couldn't remember where I had put the towel. Those little irritants kept cropping up all the time. I got all the dirty dishes into the dishwasher and noticed the clock—we have a chime clock in the living room—ringing ten clock. It had taken me almost an hour to fix that breakfast, put the dishes away, and put the dirty dishes into the dishwasher.

I decided that I would clean our bathroom, tackle a small job first. It seemed strange to be cleaning a mirror that you couldn't see into. I scrubbed the floor not knowing whether I got up the dirt or not. When the drain in the sink clogged up, I just had to leave it, because I didn't dare look for what I thought might be Drano and take a chance on something like that. I realize now that there are a lot of things that a person just can't tackle.

Next, I decided that I was going to tape my thoughts, because I couldn't write them down. I had forgotten to put a cassette tape in the machine, so that was a real challenge. We have a table full of tapes and I decided I would try two of them to find a blank tape for recording. But first, could I get them into the machine and push the right buttons? I finally found one that had something on it that wasn't too important, so I taped right over that. I hoped it would work. I had just checked the tape, but in order to rewind and listen to it, I had to take out the microphone plug. When I was through, I couldn't get the prongs of the plug back into the holes and I was at the point of frustration before I finally made the right connection. There were three or four holes, and one prong was larger than the other so I had to get the right combination in order to get it in.

I heard the mailman come, but then realized that I would have to wait until one of my sons came home for lunch in order to see what the mail had brought. It takes an awful lot of concentration to do very simple things—even common ordinary bodily functions—when you can't see what you are doing, at least to start with. I didn't want to turn the radio on, because that would take my mind off the simple things that I was doing. I went in to use the bathroom and almost fell in, because I didn't realize that I had left the lid up. I was thirsty for another cup of coffee, but decided the effort was too much, so I took a drink of water instead.

To backtrack a little, when I got up and put the blinders on, I proceeded to get dressed, which I do without even thinking every morning. Now to know which end is up on your bra, or inside out from outside in, which is the front and which is the back of your underpants and your panty hose, you have to go by the trial and error method. The difficult thing with shoes is that they don't seem to be pointed either way; you just have to put one on to see if it feels right. When I went into the bathroom I automatically flipped the light. It didn't help a bit. To brush my teeth, I had to feel the toothpaste going onto the brush—all of these things that I had taken for granted.

When my son, Peter, came home for lunch, I explained my sensitivity program to him. He "pulled my leg" a few times, pretending that he had brought friends in with him. "Stay out of Mom's purse," he warned, and a few things like that. Then he brought in the mail and read who it was from, and those that I wanted opened, he read to me. If I'd had any intimate letters, it would have been frustrating. He had to go to work for a couple of hours and asked me if he could use the car. I said, "Well I'm not going to use it, but I don't think it would hurt you to walk those four or five blocks."

He said, "Well, it's raining out."

I said, "It is not."

He said, "Go out and feel for yourself."

My next undertaking was the laundry, which I usually do between everything else. I went upstairs and forgot to count the number of steps. I got the two hampers of dirty clothes compacted into one and started down, feeling my way towards the bottom so that I would know when I came to the last step. I took the hamper down to the basement. Instinctively, I paused to turn on the light at the top of the stairs. I started to sort the laundry and had to feel each piece in order to decide whether it went on the white, or the colored, or the jeans and socks pile, a distasteful job!

Then, when I had what I thought were three piles, I went to re-check them, and I bumped into something strange and unfamiliar. One of my sons had been working with lumber, and had piled it where I usually sort my laundry. It was very frustrating and I could understand now why people who can't see don't like things changed or moved—especially my poor husband with ten of us forever moving things around. I decided that I would wait until my daughter came home to make sure that I had the right things in the right piles. There was no rush to get through with the laundry.

The phone rang again. It was my husband, and I had the same feeling of the blind talking to the blind. I hadn't told anyone, not even him, what I was doing. He asked me if I would like to go out to dinner, and I said, "Well, you don't know how smart you are, because you wouldn't get much at home. By the way," I said after telling him of my experiment, "can you tell me how to use the telephone?" I hadn't thought about that either. He told me where to start counting, and after I hung up, I tried dialing a friend's house. What a thrill! I had dialed the right number.

It was time to eat again, so I made myself a cheese sandwich. I had to slice the cheese. It came off in bits and pieces, but I put it together and had a glass of milk to which I added some chocolate. That turned out to be quite lumpy. It became quiet and lonely in the house after lunch, and I thought it must be about noon, but my watch was useless to me. I didn't know the number that I should dial for time, so I turned on the television, thinking if it were noon, it would be news time; and it was. I could envision the newscaster relating the incidents as usual about the tapes, and Watergate, and unemployment—the only thing that I missed seeing, and my imagination ran wild, was a scene of Pearl Bailey singing to the accompaniment of President Nixon at the White House. I would love to have seen the picture of that. You concentrate much more on what the newscaster is saying when you are not seeing pictures to distract you.

When I thought it was a little chilly in the house, I went over to the thermostat, but I couldn't decide whether the numbers move, or the arrow moves, when you turn the dial. I turned it a little to the right, hoping it would raise the temperature in the house. I guess it did, because the furnace went on shortly after.

A couple of times through the morning, once in the living room and once in the kitchen, I became panicky when I didn't recognize where I was. I thought I knew every inch of my house—I'd gone over it often enough with the vacuum and dustcloth. When you think you're in one place, and you reach out and touch something that isn't familiar, it frightens you because you don't have your bearings.

There was nothing that I really had to do. I tried a little dusting, but when it became complicated, like dusting a coffee table littered with magazines and books and papers, I gave up. The same with my desk. My hutch is filled with things that I would hate to break, so I let that go. Once I discovered how to dial the phone, I made several telephone calls. Not wanting to explain to people what I was doing, I fibbed a little when they asked, "Isn't it gloomy today?" Well, it was gloomy. I guess I wasn't fibbing.

The darkness and quietness were getting to me—I finally had to turn on some FM music. I was just waiting for one of the youngsters to come home—maybe we could start the laundry together. Usually I am, as they say, my own woman. I decide what has to be done and I do it. I'm very impatient. Depending on other people would really be hard for me. The humility of having to ask for help would get me down.

Time certainly dragged. I heard the chime clock strike thirty minutes after the hour—it must've been one-thirty. I listened to the Radio Talking Book for a little while. This is a closed-circuit radio station that broadcasts solely for the blind. They were reading an article on problem solving—"take one day at a time, one hour at a time"—very appropriate for my day. I was cold and decided to get a jacket from my closet. I never realized that clothes all felt the same. There were short sleeves, long sleeves, heavy woolens, light polyesters, shirts, dresses, and jackets. I finally found the one I wanted.

It would've been nice to take a nap, but I'd have had to take the bed apart and then re-make it, and that wasn't easy the first time. I decided to sit and meditate and see what else struck me during my day of blindness.

I thought of things my husband did that we took for granted. When he'd get up in the morning, I'd have his coffee ready to plug in, his juice and cereal poured or instant cereal ready to mix with hot water. Sometimes it was two eggs ready to boil, or a piece of meat to fry. He'd get up before five o'clock in the morning, and he didn't mind if I stayed in bed—in fact, I think he preferred it because I'm not a morning person. Now I could see why he got up a little earlier than I thought he had to; to make sure he wouldn't have to rush through these morning chores.

Then he took his white cane, crossed Lyndale Avenue, walked up a block and a half and caught the bus. When he'd get off downtown, usually there was another man who worked at City Hall who walked with him to his stand. When he opened up at seven o'clock it was a constant rush of people until he closed at four-thirty. They'd want him to get one of twenty-four kinds of cigarettes, one of fifteen kinds of pop, one of ten kinds of sandwiches, one of four kinds of milk, one of fifteen kinds of cigars, or they'd want change or information. He had to keep his mind on each move he made. His stand was right next to the police station, and he knew just about every policeman and sheriff,

and anyone else who worked in that department by his first
name—or he recognized his voice. Each customer gave him a
little ribbing, and he took it good naturedly.

At four-thirty Pete took his cane again and walked a block and
a half to the bus stop. It was difficult to catch the Bloomington bus
because it didn't stop unless it was waved down. Some of the
daily commuters helped him with this. He was dropped off about
a half block from our house so he didn't have far to walk. Sometimes the bus driver dropped him off right in our back walkway.

I realized that in the span of the last twenty-five years, about
the only thing I didn't expect Pete to do was drive the car. He
even did that once when I got stuck in the snow and didn't know
how to rock the car. He showed me how. Another time we got
stuck and he tried to push, until he realized that I had the back
wheels hung around a corner and no amount of pushing would
have gotten me out of that mess. He had diapered babies, warmed
and given them their bottles, done the dishes hundreds of times,
and he'd done the laundry, which I had given up on, many times.
He had vacuumed, cleaned the garage, even put together a
garage-door-opener-kit, raked the yard, and cleaned the gutters
along the roof line. (I don't watch him do that!) He had danced,
waterskiied, cross-country skiied, ice skated—all the things I
wouldn't think of doing with a blindfold on. It would terrify me to
walk across the street.

Pete had told me that after his training at the Army Hospital
and his orientation in Connecticut, he had had to pass all kinds of
tests in order to be discharged from the service. That had given
him an incentive to hurry up and learn. Many blind people walk
with their head up in the air, with a hesitant step. Very few people
who didn't know my husband would guess that he couldn't see.
We usually don't warn people ahead of time; this avoids a stilted,
over solicitous, loud conversation. Our children never warned
their friends either. They accepted their dad's blindness as
another child accepts his dad's baldness. Usually after a person
had met Pete and watched him operate, he'd say, "But he can
see a little, can't he?"

"No, he can't," I'd tell him. "He has two artificial eyes."

Finally, my son came home, re-sorted the clothes, and helped me get started with the laundry before he went to work. If a person had to do this all the time he'd have to mark the dials some way so that he would know where the dial should be set for the water temperature, the time, and the kind of material in the wash. Just going up and down the basement steps, counting thirteen steps up and thirteen steps down, had become quite a chore. I'd have to wait for someone to come home to reset the dials and start the next load. This dependence was depressing. Each time I'd put a new load in, I'd need to have someone set the dials and get it started for me. The drier I could handle, except that after the clothes were dried, I couldn't tell which should be hung on hangers or which should be folded. I piled them in a heap on the table.

I thought it would be a good day to get some telephoning done for a party my cousin and I were giving the next week. I talked to her about the menu, whom to call, the prizes, and the entertainment. I tried to take notes, and hoped I'd be able to decipher them later.

I hadn't told my children ahead of time that I was planning to do this little research on blindness, so that as each one came home from school, I explained, "No, I didn't hurt my eyes." "No, I hadn't gone to the eye doctor to have my eyes dilated." When I told them what I'd been doing all day, they began to play tricks on me—that's one of the reasons I hadn't told them ahead of time.

By four o'clock I wished that day were over—it was getting a little draggy. I'd discovered that there were ways of bending down or bending over so that I wouldn't hit my head. There were ways of bumping furniture so that I wouldn't skin my shins. I'd learned all kinds of things. I learned that blind people get a feeling of close contact when they're on the telephone. I had noticed that when other blind people called Pete, they talked on and on, and now I got the idea. They had a feeling of presence. I had a phone call asking me if I could do something the next Thursday afternoon, and being dependent upon someone else's eyes again, I had to have the calendar checked to see what I had scheduled for that day.

When my husband came home, I was so glad to see him I poured each of us a glass of wine. I spilled his as I served it, and realized with my inexperience, I should have used flat-bottomed juice glasses instead of stemware. Our dinner out was hilarious for the family, but I think we were a pitiful sight to other diners in the restaurant. I noticed a hush as we walked to our table; not too many young boys come in leading a blind father who is leading a blind mother! I had a bowl of soup and a sandwich which Pete said was a cop-out. I had another blow to my ego when I had to get into the passenger's seat of the car. You really have to trust in God and your son's driving ability; at each intersection I could imagine cars coming at us. I was actually relieved to get back home to familiar territory.

I took a bath and learned that you have to hang on to the soap. I tried to get interested in television, but the canned laughter and pantomime was frustrating. I left the blindfold on all night so that when I woke up, I couldn't look at my illuminated dial. I heard the trusty chime clock toll three quarters of the hour, and had to wait fifteen minutes to find out it was four o'clock. Only three more hours and I would be able to see again, thank God.

Chapter XXXIV

When Pete was in the army hospital, he met Father Thomas Carroll of Boston, who did much to help the men accept their loss of sight. He spent his whole life working for the rights and dignity of the blind. I used his book, *Blindness,** for much of my information. Each blind person must be considered as an individual, and his reaction to blindness will depend on his personality, inner resources, circumstances, etc. Before Pete lost his sight, he was a hard-working, neat, fun-loving, quick-witted boy, according to his mother. He had all these same qualities after he was blinded, but society pegged him with other words—blind, handicapped, and afflicted. According to Father Carroll, when a person loses his sight he also suffers twenty other losses, not one by one, but all together:

1. The first loss is the death of sight and your old way of life. This happened before I knew Pete, but from all reports he was able to accept his new life quite soon in the hospital. He has said that when he came so close to death and survived he knew God must have had some purpose for his life.

2. The loss of physical wholeness. There is so much value placed on bodily perfection that this could destroy a man's self image. Before his plastic surgery Pete's face was very disfigured; maybe it was a blessing he couldn't look into a mirror. His arms were broken so he couldn't even feel the scars. The plastic surgeons had to rebuild his nose, mouth, eyebrows, and facial skin.

* Little, Brown, & Co. Boston—1961.

3. The loss of confidence in remaining senses. There is wide-spread belief about a sixth sense that automatically appears when sight is gone. There is no increased acuteness of hearing, feeling, smelling, etc. until the blind person trains himself and develops an awareness of noises, sounds, smoke, fragrances, and touch. Pete is adept at using all his senses and no longer has to give constant attention to the simple operations of living. He smells the salt and pepper, he listens for traffic when he crosses the street each morning to go to work, and he has very sensitive touch when he is looking for something with his hands.

4. Loss of visual background. Subconsciously we are always seeing a background, but for a person who is completely blind there is no change in color, movement, or form. For Pete, it is always dark so he fills in with an auditory background, and he also has a vivid imagination and recollection.

5. Loss of light security. The public wants to relate light to sight and darkness to blindness, e.g. "darkened lives of the blind." Their agencies are called "lighthouses." Light is connected with hope, beauty, and goodness, and darkness is evil, gloom, and even death. Pete is comfortable in his "lightlessness."

6. Loss of mobility—power to walk. This was one of Pete's biggest hurdles. He wanted to be independent and go places. During his rehabilitation at Valley Forge Hospital he learned the Hoover cane technique which involves swinging the white cane from side to side and literally clearing a path ahead of himself. He traveled by himself through seven years of college, mastered seven different house plans and landscapes, and takes the bus into downtown Minneapolis every day. He walks briskly and has the scarred shins to prove it. Re-arranged furniture, doors ajar, cluttered stairways, and toys on the floor have always been taboo at our house, but there are low branches, snow, ice, and drivers turning corners and coming out of alleys. Pete has bent many canes on these impending dangers.

7. Loss of techniques of daily living. Eating, drinking, dressing, bowel and bladder functions, keeping oneself neat and clean, shaving, etc. are all necessary operations that have to be done systematically by the blind. "A place for everything and every-thing in its place" is their motto. Pete has the neatest drawers;

sox, hankies, underwear, shirts and pajamas have gone into the same place for twenty-five years. His wardrobe is arranged alphabetically according to color. In keeping with the style he has developed sideburns, and has discovered his own system for measuring them with an elastic band. I have already described his early morning breakfast routine.

8. Loss of ease of written communication. Illiteracy has been equated with ignorance; another blow to the blind person's ego. When our children were little, they wanted their daddy to read to them, and he started out faking it, but they caught on. Soon he had them telling him the stories from the pictures, and he had such a good imagination that he could tell them stories that were better than those in the books. Pete reads two or three books a week on his Talking Book record player. He also listens to the daily newspaper on his talking radio. The family reads to him, too; not only newspapers and books, but his mail, his records for his vending stand, and any information he needs for the various organizations he belongs to.

9. Loss of ease of spoken communication. It is difficult to listen to a person when you don't see his facial expression, gestures, and mannerisms. It is hard to follow a shrug of the shoulders or a nod of the head, or expressions such as "over here" or "this big." Some blind people assume an awkward posture or head movement, but Pete seems to "look" at whomever he addresses. One of his pet peeves is the guessing game, "Pete, guess who this is!" Another is people asking me whether he would like another serving, drink, or whatever. I try to smile as I say, "Why don't you ask him?" He uses Braille notes for his business, but they are not practical to use for public speaking. He has held several national offices in the Blinded Veterans Association, and at one time smashed all his Braille notes as he rapped for order.

10. Loss of informational progress; keeping up with the times. This could be a problem when a blind person lives alone or with other blind people, but Pete lives in a sighted world and knows more about what's going on than I do. His stand is at the Minneapolis Court House, across from the police department so he is surrounded by activity all day.

11. Loss of visual perception of the pleasurable. This loss per-

tains to objects that formerly or normally would be pleasing: a mother's face, a favorite picture, the old homestead, or something he owned like a new car, or even sexually stimulating objects. I think not seeing his family bothers Pete because he never mentions it.

12. Loss of visual perception of the beautiful. If a person were aware of art and beauty before he lost his sight, this would be a great loss. He would have to look for auditory beauty in nature, birds' singing, water rippling, and especially music. He would visualize from descriptions by sighted people, which sometimes can be sad. Pete is not the artistic type, and my enthusiastic rambling about a beautiful sunset doesn't excite him.

13. Loss of recreation. For an active sportsman like Pete, giving up playing football and baseball was a sacrifice. He still enjoys them as a spectator. He seeks his recreation among sighted people; therefore, he goes fishing, camping, cross-country skiing. He's tried water skiing and ice skating; we've ridden a tandem bicycle for over 15 years. He enjoys dancing, eating out, playing cards, and visiting friends.

14. Loss of career, vocational goal, or job opportunity. The dignity of working is important to any man's ego, and people with visual problems have to overcome a lot of prejudice and public ignorance in order to take their rightful place in the working-man's world. Job openings may not turn up, as in Pete's case, when he graduated with a Master's Degree in vocational counseling. He still has a file of rejections from state rehabilitation agencies all over the United States who wouldn't hire a blind man! The Minneapolis School Board would not hire a blind teacher twenty years ago. Consequently, we started our own business, a religious gift shop, and Pete did most of the selling, restocking, etc., for twelve years. Then he went into the vending stand program.

15. Loss of financial security. It is more expensive for a blind person to live if he has to take taxis, hire readers, a housekeeper, or secretary. The civilian blind have really been neglected financially, and Father Carroll suggests a public insurance through Social Security to give them the financial security they need. The blinded veterans' compensation program has proved that financial

motivation is not the only reason for a man to work. These men could vegetate at home, but the majority of them are rehabilitated and employed. It decreases their dependence upon their family when they can afford to buy services, and it gives them dignity and security.

16. Loss of personal independence. We all have a drive for independence and freedom and also a drive for dependence and protection. When a person loses his sight, he must realize that a certain degree of dependence is forced upon him, and if he is mature he will accept what is necessary. Many times family, friends, or relatives try to increase this dependence. Pete has difficulty accepting dependence, especially upon his wife. It seems to go against his Bostonian background where a gentleman protects his lady. It's hard for me as a wife, too, to keep a balance in my role as decision maker in shopping, decorating, keeping the finances, and disciplining children. There are many times when his opinion could be valuable in making a decision, but through habit, I neglect to consult him first. For twenty-five years, I have been in the driver's seat of our car and this tends to make me quite independent. Sometimes I think Pete feels that it's easier to join me than fight me!

17. Loss of social adequacy. This aspect of blindness is forced upon the blind by sighted people who treat them like a minority group, not with hatred, but with pity. They have stereotyped notions of begging with tin cups, piano tuning, and chair caning as the only capabilities of the blind. They give them free bus tickets and fishing licenses that set them apart. Pete feels he can carry his own weight financially, socially, spiritually and every other way, and all blind people should be given the opportunity to do so if they want to. People don't realize that he can rake the lawn, diaper a baby, be a delegate at a political convention. He can even be a pallbearer or best man.

18. Loss of obscurity. A blind man loses his privacy. He's noticed wherever he goes. This is especially true of those who have some disfigurement besides being blind. Pete never wore dark glasses for the first twenty years because they were a symbol of blindness. Then a fellow blinded veteran, whose face was more

disfigured than Pete's, felt his face and convinced him he should
wear them for cosmetic reasons. I think people should know he's
blind because when they see him in action, it could change the
attitude of a whole community.

19. Loss of self-esteem. Probably all the other losses would
cause this one if a person becomes blind suddenly. This self-
esteem has to be rebuilt right away, and fortunately Pete's was
while he was still in the hospital. His family traveled hundreds of
miles every week to visit him, and he had tremendous faith in God
and his fellow man. He found unknown strength, and he has an
Irish wit that has helped him surmount almost every obstacle to
rehabilitation.

20. Loss of total personality organization. Blindness is a series
of blows that can upset its victim and result in a neurotic response. His personality, strength, philosophy and goals make a
difference in how those blows affect him. Some people accept
their blindness as merely an inconvenience. This can be danger-
ous both emotionally and physically. Sometimes reality may
come much later. I think our family takes Pete's blindness for
granted, probably more than we should. Many times the children's friends play at our house for weeks before they realize Pete
can't see. Our own children accept it so casually that the attitude
is infectious.

Besides the twenty losses that occur when a person is blinded,
there may be some gains. As in the case of men blinded in service,
there were educational and vocational advantages. If Pete had
returned from the war in good health, he probably would have
gone back to his job of selling men's clothing instead of going to
college. He has had a chance to see how much goodness there is
in the world. He has discovered strengths he didn't know he had,
and he was forced to establish values. He has gained many
friendships, and as Father Carroll said, "Many blinded ser-
vicemen met wonderful girls who have since become their wives,
whom they would never have met if their blindness had not
brought them to a particular hospital." He has been blessed with
nine healthy children who love him and are proud of him. I think

he holds the world's record for the number of Show and Tell programs where he has explained Braille.

Now that I have a very minute idea of what he goes through every day, I have more admiration for him than ever. As Father Carroll said, "We must analyze blindness objectively and analytically before we can attempt to make the blinded person feel the subjective warmth of our love." This I have tried to do.

Chapter XXXV

Bless the Lord,
oh my soul,
and all my being,
bless His holy name.

Psalm 103.

How do you say thank you for the love, the children, grandchildren, the dear friends and relatives, the material and physical well-being that Pete and I had been blessed with for the past twenty-five years? It was a happy occasion and we wanted to share it with those we loved.

What better way than to celebrate the Banquet of Life which Jesus shared with all of us at the Last Supper? We had an evening mass with as many of the original wedding party as could attend. Father Dick, with a little less hair and a few more pounds than in 1949, was the celebrant again. Aunt Rosie, who had just celebrated her own golden wedding anniversary, played the same processional march, the same "Panis Angelicus" and "Oh Lord I Am Not Worthy" that she played at our wedding. Our sons, John and Paul, were altar boys; Jim, Joe, and Peter did the readings; and our daughters, Libby, Margaret, Mary Catherine, and Nellie, read the petitions asking the Lord to bless each person in the church. Our granddaughters, Christi and Cheri, brought up the offertory gifts.

When our oldest son Jim read "A Prayer for Your Anniversary" I swallowed hard.

Eternal God and Father, in the fulness of this day's joy, we turn our hearts in praise and gratitude to You. We thank You for Your favor which has preserved and sustained our parents and permitted them to reach this hour. In the midst of family, friends and loved ones, they look back in reverent and grateful reminiscence upon the span of years since first they pledged their hearts to one another and You. Many and varied have been their experiences since that hour; many have been the mingled occasions of victory and defeat, of fulfillment and disappointment. We thank You for the joys unnumbered with which You have sweetened their lives; and likewise we praise You for the trials, which, with Your help, they have surmounted. As You have blessed them in the past, so continue to bless them in the years to come. May it be Your will that these be years of health and contentment in the circle of their family and loved ones. This we ask through Christ our Lord. Amen.

During the Kiss of Peace, Clare Doble, who grew up in my hometown of Browerville, sang "Shalom." When all of our children and grandchildren came up to the altar to give us a hug, which was completely unrehearsed, I started to cry and Pete blew his nose. I heard other noses blowing throughout the church.

As Pete and I walked out during the recessional hymn, I saw my dear friend Claire from St. Cloud Teachers' College days. She and I had been close for almost thirty-five years, and now she was dying of cancer. She was sitting in the back pew, and her sunken blue eyes sparkled with joy as she smiled and waved. She used the last bit of strength she had to share in our happy day. Two weeks later she died.

After the mass we had a dinner and dance at the Knights of Columbus Hall; our children and friends had helped with the food and decorations. The tables were beautiful with blue and silver streamers, blue votive candles, a centerpiece and sprays of blue and white flowers that were given to us by our generous friend, Ardyce. She wrote, "My gift of love to you two special people is in each and every flower."

Our Irish friend, Lois Hennessey Andersen, had stitched a needlepoint shamrock with our family names, the date of our

wedding, and each of the children's names. It hangs like a coat
of arms over our fireplace. Lois has seven children, a full-time
job, and goes to college, so when she had to take "sick leave"
for a hysterectomy, she used the time to finish our anniversary
gift.

For the previous five years, Pete had told all his customers that
he was saving half dollars. "I'm taking Mary to Ireland for our
silver wedding anniversary," he'd tell them. Some of the people
must have robbed their own collections, because no matter how
scarce they were, Pete brought home as many as ten dollars
worth of halves every week. We built up our "Ireland Fund" with
them, and although we specified "no gifts" on our invitation to
our anniversary celebration, many people made generous contri-
butions, or as our friend Marie Corrigan said, gave "fur for the
kitty."

We joined the Irish American Cultural Institute in St. Paul to
get on their charter flight to Ireland leaving June 15.

Peter and Paul were going with us. We couldn't afford to stay
with the tour at one hundred and twenty dollars a day, so we
planned to "do" Ireland on our own. That was scary for novices
like us.

Our children, after much rationalizing, had given us a movie
camera and projector for our anniversary. Pete was used to this
kind of gift. One birthday, he was given a camping lantern,
another time a flashlight that floated, and many pictures and
plaques. We had even considered field glasses at one time. The
movie camera was to bring Ireland back to the rest of the family,
and with thirty rolls of film in our pack, we intended to try.

Our plane was scheduled to leave at eleven at night, but we had
to be at the airport two hours early. It was an exciting farewell
party. There were twice as many people who came to say goodbye as there were passengers—our aunts, uncles, children, and
friends among them.

Weeks before our flight we had reserved our seats. When I
asked Pete where he'd like to sit, he said, "Just make sure it's
near the restroom." We had the last seats in the tail of the plane,
and when we asked to be near the bathrooms, we didn't realize
that we would also be near the bar, the all night smokers' hang-

out, and in the path of two hundred and fifty passengers going down the narrow aisle to the toilet. We met people we knew, even relatives, as they made their way up and down the aisle.

It was a short night. By two o'clock we were into daylight, and at noon, seven hours after we left Minneapolis, we were flying over the green fields near Shannon Airport. Our son, Peter, had his eye behind the camera lens from that moment until we took off again nineteen days later. He said some day he was going back and look at Ireland without a camera in front of his face.

When the four of us picked up the car we had rented, I wanted to scrap the whole idea. Renting a car seemed so simple in the brochure. Now I sat in a Vauxhall miniature station wagon—the steering wheel was on the right-hand side of the car, there was a four-on-the-floor shift to my left, a few gadgets sticking out of the post behind the wheel, and we were parked on the left side of a two-way street.

Where should I start? I got the motor running in neutral, then I pushed what I thought was the windshield wipers to take care of the "soft mist" that was falling. Instead, the turn signals went on. I tried the other gadget and the horn beeped. It had been years since I had used a clutch in our 1947 Chevrolet, and to coordinate it with the left hand shift seemed awkward.

Learning all this in one block at the airport before we came to the highway was a trying, jerking experience. The first time we met a car, I turned toward the ditch and almost scraped the left side of the car. In fact, during most of our trip on the narrow roads, Pete, on the passenger side, had the branches hitting his elbow—I didn't want to brush with those wild drivers on my side of the car.

We spent the first night at the Ryan Hotel in Limerick where we soon learned that we would have been smarter to go to a guest house for a third of the price, with breakfast included. We also learned that after a big breakfast of eggs, sausage, cereal, juice, soda bread and marmalade, we were not ready for the Irish dinner hour at noon. Instead, we would buy a loaf of bread, some meat, cheese, and fruit, and a bottle of wine and have our own picnic in some quiet pasture.

In our itinerary, we planned to encircle most of the island, so we started north to Ennis and the Cliffs of Moher and on up into Galway. We sampled every quaint facet of Ireland on our first day. We had to stop twice while herds of cattle crossed the road; then the farmers gave us a friendly nod. We saw men, women, and children out in the bogs gathering peat for their fuel and cooking, and hauling it in their donkey carts. Everywhere we saw people on bicycles—old women, even nuns with their veils flying in the wind. The men working in the fields had suits, white shirts, and ties on, and when we inquired about it, we were told, "They're ready for the pub when it's quittin' time."

When we stopped the second night at Mrs. O'Connor's St. Joseph Guest House in Galway, we drove out to the Bay to watch the sun go down. Because it was close to the equinox, it was still light when we gave up and went to bed at eleven.

Tuesday, June 18, was election day in Ireland and the political parties, Fine Gael and Fianna Fail, had posters of their candidates nailed or pasted to every building, post, and even on trash cans. The voters came to the polls by foot, bicycle, and donkey cart.

My sister-in-law had given us the name and address of her aunt and uncle, Julia and Tom Quigley, who lived near Galway. It was difficult to find their little farm because the address just had a series of names: Springlawn, Mt. Bellow, Ballinasloe, County Galway. We at least knew we were in the right county! When we thought we were close, we sent Peter to a house to ask if they knew the Quigleys. He swung his arms motioning for us to come in; they were the Quigleys. After the shock of meeting "Nellie Donahue's relatives from America" (we really weren't related to Peggy's mother, but we didn't care to split hairs over it), they invited us to stay for a visit. Julia took us out to the potato patch to meet Tommy, her husband, and as she said, "He's seventy and sickly." On the way, we passed their chicken coop, an abandoned 1930's car without wheels. The chickens could wander in and out under the fenders.

Tom Quigley brought his donkey out of the field for Paul to sit on and have his picture taken, and as Julia said, "Sure'n it'll be hard to tell which ass is which!" Then she put turf in the range and boiled a kettle of water for tea, which she served us with fresh homemade bread. When we finished eating, Julia took us out to the bogs and explained how the turf is cut by machines and piled up to dry. She also showed us the heather that grew wild in the meadows, along the roads, and even out of rocks. When we got back it was Tom's turn for hospitality. He rode into town with us and we stopped at Kelly's Bar for a ha'guinness . . . our first taste of this much publicized Irish dew. Pete enjoyed it, but it reminded me of warm, thick, dirty oil from the crankcase of a car.

This Irish family couldn't do enough for us. Next, Julia hopped in our car and directed us to another relative of Peggy's. On the way, we stopped at a schoolhouse where she voted. At the next farm, we met eighty-year-old Mike Goley. He was blind and spent his days sitting by the cozy fire in the hearth. I will never forget the smell of that turf fire. Mike's daughter and her family treated us to Irish whiskey and biscuits. It's a good thing Peggy didn't have any more relatives over there—we'd still be eating and drinking.

By our third day, we had found the Ireland of the Welcomes—"You're welcome to stay awhile, a month, a year, forever."

My dear Irish friend, Bridget Grundy, had asked us to "stop awhile and say hello to me cousin Mike" at Glashlaun. Everybody seems to know that I'm a "people person" who enjoys visiting more than sightseeing. On the map it looked like a twenty-five mile drive off our course, which we'd be glad to do for Bridget. We drove to the coast at Clifden, then up to Letterfrack and started to inquire in various pubs for Michael Coyne. After much "arguin' and reminiscin' " among themselves, we were told where we might find him. At each pub we were directed to a different Mike Coyne—one had been dead for five years!

We finally found Bridget's cousin in a brick cottage by the sea. She had told us that she was born in a thatch-roofed cottage, but now only the foundation was left. I stood on the shore and envisioned Bridget as a little girl helping her brother catch fish for their noon meal. Mike's wife and son were home with him. All three of the Irish men we had met so far were at least twenty years older than their wives. At the Coynes' we had tea, fresh dark bread, and rhubarb pie.

Most of the time we budgeted our money very carefully, but a few times we splurged. Our night at Ashford Castle was one of them. We had sent forty-five dollars with our reservations, and it cost another sixty when we arrived. Driving through the gate and up to the stately entrance, we felt as though we were dreaming . . . an honest-to-goodness medieval castle for all night.

It was after nine when we arrived and were taken to our elegant room with brocade wallpaper and gold faucets. It was luxurious, but there were only two beds, a double and single for the four of us. We had to take the mattress off to make an extra bed. We got up early the next morning to put the room back together; we didn't want the maid to see how we shanty Irish would desecrate Ashford Castle.

When Pete and I were all ready for bed, Peter and Paul came bursting into our room, all excited, "Look who we met in the hall! The McKeens—they're from Minneapolis!"

We invited them in to our disrupted room and found out we had all come over on the same plane. Even more coincidental, Libby McKeen worked in the Richfield Library with my friend, Lois Andersen. We ran into the McKeens several other times in our tour around the country.

The next morning, after a six course breakfast that was included in the cost, we went back to the humble road and our thrifty travel budget.

For the next three days we looped up through Sligo, William Butler Yeats' country, on to Donegal, the handwoven tweed center, and back down to Roosky on the Shannon River where we stayed at Patrick and Bridie Duffy's Guest House. We told them about my Duffy relatives and hoped we were related.

In County Longford we looked up my Hoy relatives, and found one we thought had the "Hoy Look." Whenever there was any doubt we claimed to be related. At one Hoy farm we had banana sandwiches.

In Monaghan, where the bus depot had recently been bombed, we tried to find out about the McKennas. There were so many clans of McKennas in this region of Ireland that you had to know the nickname of the clan in order to trace your family origin. We met interesting McKennas in the pub and in the stores they owned, and they were all eager to be related to Americans.

On our drive down the east coast of Ireland, we stopped in Drogheda to see Oliver Plunkett's Shrine. Most of our friends had asked us to visit their relatives' homes; our friend, Eileen Roth, asked us to pay our respects to someone who had been dead for two hundred and eighty-four years. She claimed to be a relative of Oliver Plunkett, and now that he was being considered for canonization she was sure of it. We saw his skull and the jail door of his cell and said a prayer for Eileen.

When we arrived in Dublin, we felt as though we were driving in any American city, until we tried to follow the street signs and the traffic officer. The streets changed names without changing direction, so we had a difficult time finding our way around. Our guesthouse was around the corner from the American Embassy; we used the American flag as our landmark. There was a bus strike on in Dublin and the traffic and parking problems were mind boggling. We either walked several miles to the downtown area or drove as close as possible and then took a cab.

Son Peter's highlight of the whole trip was our night at the Abbey Theater where we saw "The White Headed Boy"—a tragi-comedy about a typical Irish family in the twenties, all bachelors and spinsters sacrificing for the fair-haired boy to get through medical school.

Pete and I had our own private pilgrimage to Granby Lane, the spot where Matt Talbot, an Irish drunk who took "the pledge" and kept it for forty-one years, had collapsed and died on his way to mass. Then we walked for blocks and blocks to our Lady of Lourdes Church where his remains have been entombed. A glass panel reveals his coffin, and a plaque is inscribed: "The Servant of God, Matthew Talbot, 1856-1925. People come to pray to him for sobriety, and for him, that some day he'll be a recognized saint."

From Dublin, we drove through southeastern Ireland: Glendalough, an ancient monastery, Arklow, known for its pottery, Wexford and the John F. Kennedy Park, and on to Waterford and the Crystal Factory. Here we had a personally conducted tour because they thought Pete couldn't walk on the viewing balcony. We walked right by the hot furnaces where the blowers took the hot liquid glass and formed them into goblets and vases. Then we saw the cutter put in the various patterns, Colleen, Lismore, Kylemore, and Kildare, by holding the glass up to a carburundum wheel and then to a polishing wheel. The guide told us that these workers start at age fifteen and work for five years before they can take the "test", which is cutting a perfect bowl. If they pass, they go on to journeyman, and then to master craftsman. After seeing the tedious process to produce the small honey jar that I eventually bought, I considered eight dollars a bargain price.

In south central Ireland we visited the relatives of my brother-in-law, John Brown. They had tried for a year to start a river tourist business over there, and had almost given up on the idea. We had our first real Minnesota coffee, made with egg, and we swapped stories about our adventures with the Irish people. Joan Brown said, "It takes a year to get used to the system here—or the lack of it."

We made a quick trip to Cork, the big southern port, and on to Blarney Castle to climb the one hundred and twenty winding steps to trade our kisses for the gift of eloquence just as millions of other tourists had done.

To complete our tour of the island, which is about as big as the southern third of Minnesota, we stopped at Killarney, the Dingle Penninsula, and Tralee, the most beautiful mountain and lake region in Ireland. We were lucky to be able to attend the Siamsa in Tralee, a performance of Irish folk songs, dance, and mime that depicts Irish life of long ago.

Then back up to Limerick for our last night and our banquet at Bunratty Castle. We started our medieval meal with mead, a honey wine that was thought to enhance virility; newly married bridegrooms drank it for a month, hence the "honey moon." We drank soup from a clay bowl, and ate soda bread, spare ribs, chicken, carrots, beans, and salad with our fingers, just as in medieval days. Our final course was a pinch of snuff.

We turned in our Vauxhall with slightly over sixteen hundred miles, all on the "wrong side" of the road. By this time, we had become attached to it and would like to have taken it home with us.

When we met all our fellow travelers back at Shannon Airport, it was like old home week. We swapped stories and shopped for last minute souvenirs until it was time to fly back to Minnesota. If we didn't have our twelve hundred feet of movies to show that those past three weeks were real, I'd have been afraid to wake up and end the dream.

Chapter XXXVI

Just when we thought we had plugged up all the leaks in the dike of family problems, we got a call from the city jail. It was one of our sons. He had been living with a boy who had stolen a stereo and the police picked up our boy as an accessory. They both would have to appear before the judge the next afternoon.

"Don't worry about me, Mom," he said. "It'll be OK." I had asked if we could see him or if he needed anything. "You could bring me some clean clothes."

The next day, I had the incongruous choice of going to the St. Paul Hilton for a chic style show and luncheon or going down to the county jail to see my son. Even as I prayed for guidance and strength, I knew I'd made my choice. It occurred to me that maybe my son hadn't always come first before my luncheons, my priorities and my comfort. Instead of donning my fur trimmed coat and fashion boots, I got into my everyday grocery shopping gear and hoped I wouldn't be conspicuous among the visitors.

At the window marked, "Jail passes, Monday, Wednesday, and Friday", I stood in line waiting and hoping I wouldn't see anyone I knew. I studied the faces of the other visitors. Young girl friends with open faces, pregnant wives with an anxious look, black fellows with packages of clothes just like I carried, and one very well-dressed gentleman who I was sure must be an attorney or minister visiting his client. When my turn came to sign my name, I could hardly control the pen. It was even more difficult to fill in "Relationship *Mother*." I seemed to remember a story told by my

160

third grade teacher of a criminal standing up in court and pointing to his mother screaming, "It's all her fault! If she had corrected me when I stole my first nickel I wouldn't be here today!" But I had corrected my son and had tried to teach him the values necessary for living a good Christian life.

Finally the elevator took me to the fifth floor where I was in a maze of cages. The visitors' room was a series of glass windows with metal grills, separated into stalls for a minimum of privacy. As I waited my turn, I saw visitors talking and laughing, eager to fill their fifteen minutes with all the news of the outside world. The prisoners were such ordinary looking boys and men. I heard the well-dressed gentleman talking to a young blond boy, "Your mother sends her love," and at the end, "Be good, son." So this happens to all families, all races, all economic classes.

When my turn came, I held my head up high and gave my son a big smile. He assured me that he was not involved as suspected and that things would work out as soon as the other boy would testify. He was trying to cheer me up. I threw him a kiss through the glass and assured him I'd see him as soon as possible.

By the time we celebrated our silver wedding anniversary, our teenagers had moved on up to their twenties. Jim had gone to the University of Minnesota, and with a few "dropping out" periods, was still a few credits shy of a degree in business and accounting. The girls had established themselves in apartments. In fact, the first six children had moved out of our home once, twice, or even three times to "do their own thing", whatever that meant. In the late sixties and early seventies peer support was more important than parental support—until the price of rent or groceries or laundry overwhelmed them. If four guys shared an apartment for two hundred dollars a month, it seemed like a small price for freedom until one of them moved out and the others were stuck with higher rent. Our old furniture went back and forth from apartments to our basement so many times, we finally put our foot down. "You can move back home, but don't bring that junk with you!"

It was difficult having adult children move back under my maternal wing. They had tasted independence and it was restrictive to have mother waiting up for them. "If I lived away from home, I

could be out all night and you wouldn't worry about me," they'd
retort as I complained about losing sleep. They were absolutely
right!

In October, 1974, John and Joe joined the service. They were
not certain about what they wanted to be when they "grew up"
and they needed a few years of experience, discipline, and income while they decided. John, who had gone to cooking school,
but didn't want to make a career of it, joined the army. Contrary
to what you hear about the army snafu, they put him to work in
the mess hall. He was also trained as a paratrooper in the special
forces, which pleases his dad whose own army career came to a
screeching halt against his will. John loves the army.

Joe joined the Air Force hoping to learn about electronics and
possibly aeronautical engineering. He spent two years putting gas
and oil into planes and getting them ready for take-off, but since
then has been sent to Italy and Germany for brief periods as a
crew chief.

When Joe and John left for boot camp, it was the beginning of
our family breaking away. Until this time, the children had gone
away to school or into apartments, but we were always together
for holidays, birthdays, and any other excuse. Our nest was
emptying.

We felt this loss for the first time when our daughter, Mary
Catherine, was married at Thanksgiving; her brothers couldn't be
here for her wedding. She and Scott had planned to be married
earlier in the year, but had postponed their wedding in deference
to our anniversary and trip to Ireland. This was typical of Mary
Catherine's generosity and selflessness. We tried to make up for it
by having a meaningful nuptial mass and a dinner and dance for
over two hundred and fifty relatives and friends. She and Scott
were both attending Normandale Community College so they had
to settle right in after the wedding.

Both Joe and John finished boot camp in time to come home for
Christmas. We still carried out our Christmas Eve tradition and it
had grown through the years. As we sang "O Come All Ye Faithful" and carried the Christ Child, the lighted candle, the Family
Bible, and a chalice of wine into the living room, the youngest
grandchild put the babe into the manger. I read aloud the Gospel

of St. Luke telling the story of the birth of Jesus in Bethlehem, we sang "Silent Night", we all drank a toast from the chalice of wine, and finally, we sang "Happy Birthday" to Jesus. Each year our procession from the kitchen to the living room would get a little longer, with sons-in-law and grandchildren. We added stockings on our fireplace for Fred, Christi, Cheri, and now, Scott. Soon we would have to layer them!

When Joe, who was nineteen at the time, announced that he and Diane, his high school sweetheart, were going to get married while he was home at Christmas, we didn't take him too seriously. Pete and I pointed out all the reasons they should wait until spring or next summer; they seemed agreeable. Two days before he was to go back to Texas, I read in the morning paper under Marriage License Applications: Joseph Francis McKenna . . . Diane Teresa Harwood . . . I hadn't believed that they were really going through with it, until now. Legally, they were adults; but so young. Diane's folks were less than enthusiastic about the marriage, too.

How do you get ready for a wedding that's tomorrow? After two daughters' weddings, I had looked forward to being "the mother of the groom" where I wouldn't have to make a decision or lift a finger, just go and enjoy. I called our priest, but he explained that the Catholic Church would no longer marry teenagers without a three month preparation. Pete said he knew some judges at the court house, but God forbid! Married by a judge? Our good Catholic family? I shrank two sizes at the thought. As it turned out, most of them were enjoying a recess the week between Christmas and New Year's. Joe finally found one through a friend. I had to accept it. This was their life.

Diane's mother took her shopping for a dress; girls didn't wear dresses that year, but Mrs. Harwood didn't want her to wear her jeans for this occasion. I reserved a table for dinner at the American Legion Club, and Joe got the wrinkles out of his uniform.

By two o'clock we all met in the judge's chambers. Thanks to our daughter Margaret's thoughtfulness in stopping at the florist's on the way downtown, the bride had a corsage and the groom a boutonniere. The ceremony was brief—three minutes, to be exact. Joe and Diane were just as happy as Pete and I had been after our hour long High Mass, and I had to be happy, too. Everything happened so fast I couldn't believe I was going along with it. When the newlyweds came home the next July, we all gathered at Assumption Church to have their marriage blessed.

Each of our children is unique, and we're getting used to the idea that our dreams and ambitions for them are different from theirs.

The Sunday after I thought I had adjusted quite well to Joe and Diane's sudden marriage, was Peter III's seventeenth birthday. He read an article to me in the Family Section of the *Sunday Tribune* on the disadvantages of having children after age thirty-five: not being young enough to be pliable, being the only grandmother in the PTA, and not having enough energy to cope. He shoved the article at me and said, "Mom, do you realize you were over thirty-five when I was born? According to this article, I'm a disadvantaged child!"

That was all the challenge I needed. A few phone calls and I had our whole family, including grandchildren, off to the hills for sliding. Not one of them knew how to take a running start and belly flop on the sled at a breakneck speed. I showed my granddaughters how to make angels in the snow, and how to "cut the pie" to play cat and rat. After an exhilarating afternoon on the hill, we came home and had a winter picnic on the floor in front of the fireplace. We warmed our toes as we ate his birthday cake and sang our favorite songs. When I suggested we could all hike to the drug store for ice cream, the birthday boy protested, "Mom, you've proved your point. Old mothers are really neat!"

Chapter XXXVII

One Tuesday afternoon, shortly after our family sliding party, I was working at the Birthright Office in downtown Minneapolis when a good-looking young black man walked in. I was a little startled because very few men come in alone.

"Good afternoon, Madame," he greeted me with a slightly British accent. "I have come to seek help for my wife. She is expecting a baby and we do not have the finances to pay. She was having problems and I took her to the county hospital in an ambulance and they sent me a bill for forty dollars." He laughed nervously, "I don't have forty dollars."

"I'm sure we can help you, sir. Let me fill out this sheet with the information we need. What is your name, please?"

"Bona Egbufoama," he answered with a smile. He knew I was going to ask him to spell it . . . everyone did.

"B-o-n-a E-g-b-u-f-o-a-m-a. My wife's name is Dorothy," he added. "That you can spell."

Then Bona told me his story. Sometimes I couldn't understand his fast, clipped style of speaking, and some words were unfamiliar to me, but he was patient and so was I. He had come to Minneapolis from Nigeria to learn banking and finance under the sponsorship of a Nigerian businessman. For the past year, he had been attending Metropolitan Junior College where his tuition was paid, but there was not enough money to include living expenses, much less the luxury of having his wife with him. Dorothy had stayed in Nigeria with their two children until Bona earned enough money in a factory to send for her. His parents looked after their two children when she left.

Now Bona had to give up his job because he couldn't work the night shift, go to school all day, and keep up with his studying. Being in the United States on a student visa, he couldn't get a social security card and it was difficult to find a daytime job without it. Once in a while he could wash dishes or do janitorial work, but this was not enough to pay their rent or even buy food.

When Dorothy was told they weren't eligible at the county hospital, they went to a family social agency, which suggested that she solve their problem by having an abortion. Neither Bona nor Dorothy wanted that kind of solution. In Nigeria children were still an asset, and they were anxious to have another child.

I was able to make arrangements through "Project Life" to take care of Dorothy's medical expenses—clinic visits, delivery, and postpartum care—at St. Mary's Hospital. She got maternity and baby clothes from Birthright, and free food from the nearest church-sponsored Food Shelf. The Marian Council Knights of Columbus helped with their rent until Bona found a part-time job at the college.

Because they had no telephone, Bona expressed their gratitude for these material favors in a letter:

Dear Mrs. Mary McKenna,
   It has really been a big pleasure meeting and knowing a woman of rare quality like you. Your great help time without number have given me much food for thought. You cannot imagine what you have so far done for me, financially or otherwise. I am very grateful and I am sure the Almighty will never fail to reward you.
   My wife and my brother have joined me to extend our sincere greetings and best wishes to your good and beloved husband, who is not only a friend indeed, but a friend in need. Our greetings also to all the members of the holy family. We have never failed to put you in our prayers and we hope you do the same for us. Thanks, Bona Egbufoama.

Bona's brother, Martin, had also come to the United States for his education, and they all shared one small apartment. They ate only once a day to conserve on the food they received. Even when we invited them to our house for dinner, they were unable to eat a full meal.

By driving Dorothy to her clinic appointments, she and I became good friends. She was a very quiet girl, but she smiled a lot. In Nigeria she had been a seamstress, but now she had very little material to work with. She was a meticulous housekeeper, and enjoyed reading the magazines I brought each month.

When the time came for her delivery, I was honored to be called to the labor room. In Nigeria, the grandmother stays with the mother—Bona had told the nurse that I was the "grandmother." In fact, this couple was the same age as my own children. It was a thrill for me to welcome this beautiful curly-haired black baby girl into the world. I had hoped she would make her entrance into America on the Fourth of July, but she was two days late. They called her Shirley Adazey (a blessing). They felt that she would give them a life-long bond with America; we felt we had a life-long bond with Shirley, our godchild.

The wife of the doctor who delivered Shirley donated a beautiful christening dress, and we were proud to be a part of the baptismal ceremony at St. Olaf's Church. Our family joined us for a christening party at our house, and they were all thrilled with their new adopted "niece."

After Shirley's birth we received a letter from Bona's parents in Nigeria thanking us for "the profound kindness which you show. . . . We very much appreciate the God-sent kindness being meted out to our needy ones over there. You are playing the role of father and mother on our behalf and for that we pray the Almighty God to reward you a hundredfold." We felt humble and fortunate to be able to share their kindred spirit.

When "our baby" was six weeks old, Bona had to go to Corpus Christi, Texas, to register at Texas A & T University. "We will take our possessions and go on the Greyhound Bus," he explained. I knew he had no idea how far Texas was from Minnesota, and how difficult it would be for Dorothy trying to care for a new baby for two and a half days—and nights. They knew no one, and had no place to go when they would arrive in Corpus Christi. I asked Bona about the bus fare. "It is $87.00 for each of us. I have saved enough. The baby rides free." My mind started working. There must be a better way. "Bona," I started my plan, "if you could go to Texas alone on the bus, Dorothy and Shirley could stay with us until you find a place to live. Then we will add the extra money for her to take a plane to Texas. Would you agree to that?"

When he thought about the trip, the distance, and the baby he agreed that it would be hard for Dorothy. He nodded in agreement, "You people are too good."

When I drove Bona to the bus depot, he had boxes with baby gear, pots and pans, and suitcases with everything they owned, except for what Dorothy and Shirley would need when we set them up in our guest room. They were very easy to have around—Dorothy smiled as she went along with me to the stores and friends' houses to visit.

When Bona arrived in Corpus Christi, he wrote: "I am happy I am writing you again after my safe arrival, in a foreign land . . . It took me two days to get a place to stay. I was staying with the Salvation Army which gave me everything I needed . . . I am happy you are staying well with my family. I don't know really how to thank you, but the Almighty will take care of the good things you have done to me so far. I have one request which I make and that is—I hope you people remember my family in prayers always. Sincerely yours, Bonaventure Egbufoama."

Two days later he called and asked us to send Dorothy and Shirley on the plane.

After they got settled in Texas we received many beautiful letters and cards from them. They sent photographs of our godchild and told us of her progress in eating, walking and talking. Once or twice they called us.

When Bona graduated on December 17, 1976 (my birthday), we wanted to be there, but it was impossible at Christmas time. Last winter, when we visited our son, Joe, and his wife, Diane, in Austin they drove us down to Corpus Christi to see "our family." They had surprised us a few months earlier by announcing the birth of another baby girl, Toni, so we had much to talk about.

After twenty years of camping, Pete decided he would like to buy about five acres of land on which to park our tent trailer

permanently. Each time I drove him to a campsite, I had problems. "Just swing it around to the right," the man would say as I
tried to back into a spot.

"Turn what around?" I'd ask. "The trailer or the steering
wheel?" Several times the trailer jack-knifed and I'd put a dent
into the front end of it.

We toured the counties to the south and west of Minneapolis
looking for land, but it was hard to find. With the new water and
sewer regulations, farmers couldn't sell off five acres for a "rec-
reational vehicle."

When I saw a cabin advertised on Lake Ann, about fifty miles
west, I called Pete at work.

"Why don't you drive out to look at it?" he suggested. "You
mean today?" "Sure. You could pick up your cousin Adeline on
the way. She knows all about lakes and fishing."

When we met the real-estate lady at the lake, there were two
other parties looking at the cabin. It was a cozy log cabin with a
fireplace, two bedrooms, a kitchen, and a room for a bathroom
which wasn't in. There was a pump outside and a little house,
with two holes, at the end of a path. The other prospective buyers
said they'd make up their minds the next day.

When I told Pete about the cabin, he wanted to go out that
same evening. I felt like the little pig who went to the orchard
early in the morning to outmaneuver the wolf. We drove back,
and although we couldn't get inside the cabin, we could sit on the
redwood settee while the sun was setting on the lake. The reflec-
tion was beautiful, the air calm and quiet, and without hesitation
Pete said, "Let's buy it!"

We stopped at the real-estate office that night with our earnest
money. With more loans from my folks and Pete's insurance, we
bought his permanent campsite. We parked our camper on the lot
to give us more sleeping space—our immediate family wouldn't
fit in the cabin.

In the last two years, we've had many fun weekends with relatives and friends. It's close enough to drive out for just a day, and
I've found it's a good place to run away from the noise and bustle
for a quiet time to think.

Chapter XXXVIII

My house is full of eagles; they're in the design of my wallpaper, they're handcarved in plaques, and molded into metal trivets. My children accuse me of waging a one-woman campaign to keep the bald eagle from becoming extinct. I'm unashamedly proud of the American symbols of freedom, my eagles and the flag that flies in our yard. I can cry when I hear "The Battle Hymn of the Republic", really weep over the "Taps", and get choked up every Memorial Day, Fourth of July, and Armistice Day. The promise of an entire year of bicentennial celebrations left me as excited as our early patriots.

I remember how proud I was every Memorial Day when my father donned his Word War I uniform. I'd watch in amazement as he wound the leggings and put on the breeches and jacket. He wore it for the last time of his life to celebrate the Bicentennial Veterans Day. As a Junior American Legion Auxiliary member I'd had the privilege of carrying one corner of the flag in the parade. When we stopped at the creek to honor the "sailor dead", we'd toss flowers into the water. I'd watch them float away as a minister pronounced a prayer. I figured all the dead sailors drowned, so why do the flowers stay on top? Later, at the cemetery, we four young girls held the flag under the men who fired the rifles, and as I saw my younger brothers dash to retrieve the blank shells, I was mortified that they could be so irreverent. One year, when my dad was the Post Adjutant, I was chosen to give the Gettysburg Address. I still remember the words.

Every Memorial Day since we moved to Minnesota, we have gone to Fort Snelling National Cemetery to pay our tribute to the men who are buried there. We have tried to make this a meaningful pilgrimage for our children. Some day, perhaps their mother and father will be among the crosses "row on row."

Fourth of July parades have always been a thrill for me, and every time they allowed local talent there were three McKenna kids as "The Spirit of '76." When the children played in the Assumption band we traveled all over south central Minnesota to watch them.

Armistice Day, or now Veterans Day, seems to be a sad holiday, maybe because it's a prelude to winter; the days are getting shorter, the leaves are all gone from the trees, and there's usually a damp chill in the air. For the four years we lived in Washington, D.C., I always went to Arlington National Cemetery to watch some dignitary lay a wreath at the Tomb of the Unknown Soldier. One year, I stood right next to General George Marshall.

Now, in 1976, we could proclaim our love for our country and it would be the "in" thing to do. As my contribution to the bicentennial, I compiled the one hundred year history of our parish, Assumption Church. It was a challenge, especially since the early records were written in German. I read thirteen hundred Sunday bulletins to glean the material—the fact that one lady had saved every one of them was a miracle.

Nellie had her sixteenth birthday at the beginning of the bicentennial year and that meant she could start dating just as her sisters had. And just as I did for them, I stayed awake until she came in at night, even though she'd go out the door saying, "Don't wait up for me!" One night in particular, as the chime clock tolled the hour, I realized that it was two o'clock in the morning and Nellie wasn't in yet. I lay motionless trying not to awaken Pete for there was no need for both of us to keep the vigil. My eyes watched the dancing shadows of car lights on our bedroom wall. My ears were attuned to the heavy stillness of the night, occasionally broken by the distant rumbling of a semi on the freeway, the neighbor's son coming home on his motorcycle, and the incessant chiming of the clock.

This was so unlike Nellie. Usually she called if she was going to be even a few minutes late. I had her evening's schedule in my mind and I kept going over it: the dance would end at midnight; Mike, Nellie, and the couple with them would go to Shakey's for pizza, an hour at the most. The drive home would take only fifteen minutes, if they came straight home. Where could she be? Who could I call? My imagination knows no bounds when I start worrying. Suppose they'd had an accident? I had heard a siren about an hour before—could it have been an ambulance or a police car? Could they have driven to the local lovers' lane? Heavens! Nellie? Never!

Lovers' lane—my mind shifted into reverse about forty years. I was sixteen, just like Nellie. Our class had gone to St. Cloud, about seventy miles away, for a tour of the quarries, the paper mill, reformatory, and teachers' college. At the end of the day, my girl friend, two fellows and I decided to stay in St. Cloud to see a movie. It never occurred to us that our folks would be worried. It was two-thirty in the morning when we drove into Browerville. Three cars were parked on the main street, and, as we arrived, the doors were flung open by my father, my girl friend's father, and the superintendent of schools! As I was shepherded home I was grilled, "Where?—Why?—What?—" No one believed that we really only went to a movie and came right home! I was once again standing between my mother and father waiting for the sentence to be handed down . . . like a month of staying home at night.

The lights on the wall brought me out of my reverie; there was the sound of a car in our driveway, and the hushed goodnights and car doors slamming. Nellie's home! I scrambled out of bed and stumbled on the telephone I had put next to the bed. It was off the hook!

"Mom, I've been trying to call you for an hour to tell you we stayed to clean up the hall at school after the dance."

Both my parents and I had earned our gray hair.

My mother had a special thrill this bicentennial spring when she was selected Browerville's Senior Citizens' Queen. It was a well deserved honor as she and my dad had spent most of their adult lives serving the needs of their community. Way back in the thirties, about the same time my father was the mayor, she was the president of the PTA. She went back to teaching to help out during World War II and stayed at it until she was almost seventy years old. For years, she commuted one hundred and twenty miles a day to summer school, and she finally got her degree at age fifty-five.

Our family drove to Browerville for the Bicentennial Parade, and as Queen Grandma John rode by in a convertible, her rooting section gave her a lusty yell.

The Fourth of July was the climax of celebrations. We watched the television spectacular from New York harbor, Philadelphia, and Washington, D.C. We had our own family spectacular by ringing our patio bell for ten minutes.

I've tried the Big Time: the New York World's Fair, Glen Echo in Washington, D.C., the Minnesota State Fair, and Excelsior Amusement Park where I took all the kids as soon as school was out every summer to cash in their good grades for free rides. Now, as a special birthday treat for my granddaughters, we spent the day at the new Valley Fair Park. We rode the merry-go-round, the ferris wheel, the bumper cars, but I sent them alone on the scarier rides and dives through the air. I sat on a bench, trying to match the excited faces with the sound of "Hi, Gramma!" as they whirled past. I felt that none of these technological, pre-planned, sterile, geometrically perfect parks could compare with the carnival that came to Browerville every summer.

For weeks before their arrival, I'd scrounged for money—I'd sold cucumbers to the pickle factory, picked up empty whiskey bottles in the alleys and sold them to bootleggers, and had visited my grandpa more often 'cause he'd always dig to the bottom of his long black money pouch to give me a nickel.

The trucks and crew had arrived two days early to set up the tents and rides. I'd never seen a circus parade back then, but I don't think it could have intrigued me more than those sun-baked, tattooed men who with sledge hammers and wrenches had transposed an empty block into a carnival wonderland.

The opening night I'd spend every cent I had saved. The merry-go-round, with its never ending calliope music grinding away from suppertime 'til midnight, had whirled me around through space until familiar faces had become a blur. The ferris wheel had been even more challenge, especially if it had stopped while I was at the top, or if my older brother were with me and he had rocked the seat. I would have chosen very carefully the "games of chance"—should I try for a Kewpie doll, a pillow cover printed with fancy lettering for "Mother", or a flashy ring? Mostly, I never had won anything. The excitement of that first night had always been dampened when I'd had to be home by ten o'clock. I'd felt persecuted because some of my friends could stay 'til it folded.

The second night, I'd had to hit my dad for money. With seven children holding out their grubby, grasping hands, he could only dole out a quarter to each of us. No matter, it had been just as much fun watching other people spend their money. Once in a while, if you'd kept your eyes to the ground, you might have found a nickel or dime. I'd cheer the young farm boy who hit the anvil hard enough to ring the gong. Sometimes, if he didn't have a girl friend, he'd give me the stuffed animal he had won. I loved to watch the boxing match that had been promoted each night between the carnival "strong man" and our hometown talent. The barker would have the crowd stirred up to the point that they would've yelled "Kill him!" to our fighter. I had never gone into the girlie shows, but it had seemed a mystery to me why the men had always sidled into the tent looking guilty.

Many nights I'd forgotten to go home—the noise, the colorful lights, the fascinating gypsy fortune tellers, the loud persuasive barkers had kept me in a suspended never-never-land. Such things as a ten o'clock curfew had never crossed my mind until someone would yell, "Hey, Mary, your mother and dad are looking for you!"

By the end of the week the carnival had seemed to be planted on that block, as though it had always been there. The grass had been worn to bare earth. And the litter! Those were the days when everyone tossed refuse to the ground without feeling guilty—paper cones that had held voluptuous cotton candy, candy bar wrappers ground into the dirt, empty pop bottles, which we had retrieved and sold, and bits of the streamers that had decorated the booths—all had been lying in complete abandon. I had felt sad when the tents and machinery had been torn down to move on. It was many years later before I understood why my parents were always relieved when the carnival had left town.

"Gramma, can we have a dollar for cokes?" A DOLLAR? That brought me back to Valley Fair in a hurry. A dollar would've lasted me all week!

By the end of 1976, even I had to admit that the Spirit of '76 was a bit overdone, especially the commercialism. I keep wondering what became of those millions of "Made in Hong Kong" trinkets that were so soon obsolete.

As the end of the year approached, our family planned a big homecoming for Christmas. Joe and Diane were coming from Texas, John from North Carolina, and all of our Minnesota based family would stay here. As our children moved from the teens to the twenties, they latched on to family traditions and really enjoyed being together. I remember that someone, probably a wise old mother, used to tell me when my children were little, "They may fight and argue now, but wait 'til they grow up!" I was beginning to believe her; as adults, our children really liked each other!

Chapter XXXIX

Requiescat in pace, Daddy.

> *As with leaves that grow on a vigorous tree:*
> *one falls off and another sprouts—*
> *so with generations of flesh and blood;*
> *one dies and another one is born.*
>   *Sirach 14:18.*

When I kissed my father goodbye at the door of the airplane two days before Christmas, I said the usual parting cliche, "Have a good flight, Daddy!" Five minutes later he had reached his destination. He had bought a round trip ticket to Fort Wayne, Indiana; he took a one-way trip to Heaven.

My dad purchased his ticket a month before the flight; he was a provident man. He was always ready for the next day or the next season. When he had seven young children, they all had overshoes before the leaves were off the trees in the fall. For a month he had prepared for this trip. He had helped my mother get their Christmas cards out early, had the gas company check the furnace to prevent any breakdown while they'd be gone, and he had brought his finances up to date, paying current bills and listing everything he'd need for his upcoming income tax report.

It had been thirty years since they had spent Christmas with their priest-son, the year he was ordained. Now they were going to celebrate his thirtieth jubilee with him.

When I met them at the bus depot the day before their flight, I knew Daddy wasn't feeling well. He usually grabbed the luggage and was eager to get to our house. This time he wanted to sit and have a cup of coffee. He said he'd had the flu for a few days and it had left his legs numb. He rested all afternoon and went to bed early that evening. When he said he'd had chest pains with the flu I asked him if he'd seen the doctor.

"No, I was too busy getting ready for the trip."

Did he anticipate that the doctor would forbid him to travel? I watched him climb the stairs that night, holding on to the rail, taking one halting step, bringing the other foot up, then taking another. This was so unlike my dad who always ran rather than walked. Our house was at the top of a hill and I remember as a child trying to keep up with him; my chubby legs were no match for his sprightly gait.

When we arrived at the airport I offered to get a mechanical cart for him to ride to Gate 48, but he insisted on walking. It was a long, slow walk, and at the gate I asked the agent if my parents could board early to avoid a long wait in the Christmas crowds. When their name was called I walked to the plane with them.

Later, my mother told me that after they had found their seats and had settled in, waiting to be airborne, they had started to read their well-worn daily prayer cards. When she handed him "A Prayer for Priests" he didn't reach out for it. It was one of many routine reactions they had come to take for granted after fifty-six years of marriage. She turned to see why he didn't respond and had barely called his name when the flight crew was there with an oxygen mask. In a moment they laid him in the aisle and administered cardiac pulmonary resuscitation. While they worked to save him, a fellow passenger took my mother to the rear of the plane and asked if she'd like to pray with her. Somebody else produced a Bible and read meaningful passages. It was man's concerned, loving humanity to man, and all strangers.

My dad was gone immediately, but the ambulance took him to the hospital for a doctor's confirmation of death. The airport police drove my mother to the hospital, stopping to pick up my daughter, Nellie, on the way. That morning when Nellie had helped her grandfather put on his overcoat, she had warned him not to get fresh with the stewardesses—at least not in front of grandma! They had that kind of friendly bantering relationship. At the hospital my mother felt the same warmth from the minister, the emergency room personnel, and from the priest who came to give the last blessing of the Church. The strength God gave her during that first shocking hour was an inspiration to the rest of us who were falling apart. All I could think of was the prayer of St. Theresa:

> *Let nothing disturb thee;*
> *Let nothing dismay thee;*
> *All things pass:*
> *God never changes.*
> *Patience attains*
> *All that it strives for,*
> *He who has God*
> *Finds he lacks nothing.*
> *God alone suffices.*

My mother had been praying that he would go first and not have to suffer; in Rose Kennedy-like stoicism she was saying that when God answers your prayers you shouldn't complain!

The next morning United Airlines sent two men to our house. The first one brought the luggage which had traveled to Fort Wayne and back. The second one came to offer condolences from the company and a full refund for their tickets: no charge for holding up the flight or for the first aid.

The next day, Christmas Eve, I dreaded having to go through the usual family traditions. My two sons were home from the service and we had been looking forward to having all nine of our children and their families with us. We had long distance calls, people dropping in with food and tokens of love, funeral arrangements to make, and a brother to meet who was fortunate to get a flight from Washington, D.C. My oldest brother, Father Dick, sadly carried on in Fort Wayne with the jubilee mass and dinner which my parents had meant to share, and then drove almost six hundred miles to be with us on Christmas Eve. My sister came with her family, and we had the warmest, most meaningful mass in our family room with twenty-three of us gathered around my mother and praying together, no one doubting that Grandpa was right there with us.

With the Christmas rush two of my other brothers couldn't fly in, so they drove; one from Ithaca, New York, and the other from Milwaukee. This way they were able to bring their families. We had never been together at Christmas before. Typically, Daddy left us at a convenient time, when his children and grandchildren could come without missing school. It also gave us four days to get ready for the funeral. The funeral director came one hundred and fifty miles to bring my dad back to Browerville, his home.

Through these days of Christmas I felt everything that was happening was unreal; I was dreaming and I would eventually wake up. It wasn't until the family stood around the casket and prayed "Our Father, who art in heaven, hallowed be thy name" that it struck me. This earthly body was no longer our dad. "Like olive shoots around your table" seven children and twenty-three grandchildren were praying *to* him.

The funeral was beautiful. There were twenty-five priests and brothers present. Once again, Aunt Rosie played the organ and a friend sang "How Great Thou Art" and "Battle Hymn of the Republic." Catholic funerals usually are not noted for their eulogies, but this time my father's life story was told, and we were proud: from his humble birth in a log house, his limited education—six winters in grade school and three winters in business college—his overseas service in World War I, his combined forty-nine years of service to his community as postmaster, councilman, mayor, city clerk, school board treasurer, and as many years or more of service to his church. Most importantly, we remembered his dedication to his family, raising children during the Depression, giving them the financial and moral support to earn thirteen college degrees, including one for his wife.

After the eulogy, a grandson read from the Book of Sirach:

> *The Lord sets a father in honor over his children;*
> *a mother's authority he confirms over her sons.*
> *He who honors his father atones for sins;*
> *he stores up riches who reveres his mother.*

He who honors his father is gladdened by children,
and when he prays he is heard.
He who reveres his father will live a long life;
he obeys the Lord who brings comfort to his mother.
My son, take care of your father when he is old;
grieve him not as long as he lives.
Even if his mind fail, be considerate with him;
revile him not in the fullness of your strength.
For kindness to a father will not be forgotten,
it will serve as a sin offering—
it will take lasting root.

Sirach 3:2.

Granddaughters asked for prayers of thanksgiving for his beautiful life, and younger granddaughters carried up the offertory gifts. Eight grandsons proudly and carefully held the casket as the American Legion gave their last salute, folded the flag, and gave it to my mother.

Because of the minus forty-five degree wind chill, we asked only the immediate family go to the cemetery. As each one of us said a final farewell and sprinkled his sturdy oak coffin with holy water, the droplets turned immediately to ice. This was so unlike my father; he was a warm person. But he also did everything the hard way. He didn't need to plant a large garden after his children were gone, but he still planted, canned, and froze vegetables for us; he didn't need to take care of the neighbors' winter paths, but he cleared the sidewalks of the whole block with his snow blower; he didn't need to wear outdated suits and give money to his grown children; he didn't need a beautiful June day for his funeral.

It was most difficult to give him up graciously. When you're over fifty and suddenly realize that you're not always going to be someone's child, it is a shocking and growing experience. But how fortunate that he lived for eighty-three years and one month. He grew old with dignity and good health to the very last week, and with God's goodness he was able to die with his shoes on.

One night as I lay awake thinking about my father, I got up and scribbled these lines:

I probably asked you when I was four
Now, fifty years later, I'm asking again—
What's Heaven like, Daddy?
You've been there a week now—
Or don't they have weeks?
Or days and nights?
Do you sleep?
What do you do all day?
Are there things to fix?
And flowers to tend?
Have you found your mother?
Your father? My friends, Claire and Edna?
Can you play cribbage with your friends?
Can you talk to people like Abraham Lincoln or Moses?
I hope you can be busy.
But if there's not enough for you to do up there
Ask God if you can still take care of us;
We'll always need you—
to fix things.

Chapter XL

So many times recently I have read about the meaninglessness in the lives of people going through the empty-nest stage of their lives. Some women, especially, who have devoted themselves completely to the care and feeding of their children, find themselves in a near fatal case of the blahs. They can honestly ask, "Is this all there is?"

As each stage of our family life passed—or is still passing—I have felt revitalized. Washing my last diaper, going to my last Brownie fly-up, serving that last school lunch, or taking my last child for his driver's test has been a thrill, albeit a relief, for me.

Times change, and with it, the family. I used to fantasize wildly about having eighty-one grandchildren running through my house! Now I'm wondering if I'll ever have a replacement for the original nine. When I came from a funeral recently where six grandsons were pall bearers for their grandmother, I remarked how nice it would be—.

"Don't worry, Grandma," my son-in-law piped up, "by the time you go, granddaughters will be pall bearers!"

Back in the fifties, we paid one hundred and twenty-five dollars to our obstetrician and fifty to sixty dollars to the hospital above our hospitalization coverage each time we had a baby. Now it costs about $2000. It staggers my mind to hear that it costs about $64,000 to raise a child! Besides the financial strain, young couples now have a more difficult time establishing a family be-

cause of modern trends in society. Marriage expectations have
changed so that the bride doesn't automatically become the
homemaker. She has her own career, and babies don't always fit
into her plans. I am glad that I didn't have to make the choice; we
left our family planning to the good Lord. I believe, like Carl
Sandburg, "A baby is God's opinion that the world should go
on." Just recently I read that the nation's economists are excited
about a new jump in the birth rate. The peanut butter and toy
manufacturers had been feeling the pinch. Many women in their
thirties are deciding "it's not such a bad idea to have a kid after
all."

Besides the $576,000 ($64,000 per child), we have invested our
time, our work, and our love. Raising a family wasn't easy, but
most things that are worthwhile involve a struggle. There were
happy moments, but also not-so-happy moments. When all the
children were little, sometimes it seemed that I couldn't see beyond the diapers, the clutter of the toys, the thirty-three meals a
day, and mostly, the lack of freedom. Now I can see that all these
things built our togetherness as a family. As the family meal,
especially on Sundays, has deteriorated because of sports, open
businesses, etc., I am grateful that we sat down together at five-
fifteen every evening.

By the time Pete celebrated his tenth anniversary at his vending
stand in Minneapolis City Hall, he felt that his future was fairly
secure. The State Business Enterprises for the Blind uses the
seniority system, and Pete's name was moving up on the list. Our
living expenses, with only three children living at home, should
have been dwindling, but with inflation the grocery bill stayed the
same—only the number of bags decreased.

When Pete came home with some glum news about our future,
I was shaken. "Well, I got the word today—and it doesn't look
good."

"What do you mean?"

"They're going to remodel City Hall and the plans call for a
tunnel to be built right through my stand."

"How can they do that to you? Won't they find you another
spot in the building?"

"They plan to have more vending machines and I might get those, but I don't think I'd like filling machines all day. I like working with people."

"You're good with people, too, Pete. It seems that every time we feel pretty safe, something happens to change our life."

"Well, I'm not sure that's all bad. Every change we've made so far has been for the best."

"That's for sure. Maybe it's time you looked for something different. Maybe the job market for blind people is better now. How much time do you have left at your stand?"

"They say two months, but I doubt if they'll move that fast. I guess it wouldn't hurt to look around for something else. The BVA field representative suggested some possibilities last time he was in Minneapolis."

I dug out the dusty resumes and freshened them up a bit with up-to-date data. Most of the job possibilities that we heard about were with the Veterans Administration, so Pete contacted Mr. Will Long in Washington, D.C., himself a blinded veteran. He came to Minneapolis a few weeks later and talked to the Fort Snelling VA Center about a job for Pete. We prayed and sweated and waited through the application, the interview, the oral test, and finally, many weeks later, his acceptance. He would be a veterans' benefits counselor; after twenty-three years he would finally be able to use his master's degree in counseling!

It was a challenge. At fifty-three a blind man doesn't learn a new bus route, the technology of a communications system, a completely foreign government jargon, plus a four inch thick manual of regulations that change each month, without straining all his resources. With patience from his co-workers, inspiration from the Holy Spirit, and faith and love from his family, he has overcome. He is completely happy in his new field. Every time a door has been closed for us, the entrance to a new life has been good.

Another door was opened for me, too.

Now that my family no longer needs the bulk of my time, I am free to pursue my own interests. I have taken several creative writing courses, and was encouraged when I published several magazine articles. When my last child entered school, I hadn't learned to say "no", and I became a professional volunteer. As a Friendly Visitor for Minneapolis Age and Opportunity Center, I met Bertha and Louis who became a part of our family until they died. Every week for the last eight years I helped our priest when he went to a nearby nursing home to say mass. About the same length of time I have done counseling and pregnancy testing for Birthright. Along with these commitments, I delivered Meals-on-wheels, provided transportation for the Volunteer Emergency Assistance Program, and was involved in our parish as president of the council, as a member of the Social Action Committee, and, lately, as a Eucharistic minister. I felt as though I was going in too many directions as I asked myself, "Is this what I want to do for the next ten or twenty years?"

Six months ago I heard of CPE—Clinical Pastoral Education—a course of study that sounded like it would integrate my life experiences with a training that would develop my awareness, my insight, and my ability to be a better minister to persons in a crisis. After three months of the basic course, I feel that I have barely touched the tip of the iceberg in learning the process of inter- and intra-personal relationships, but I'm on my way.

With continued inspiration from the Holy Spirit, the gift of good health, and the loving support of our family, Pete and I are both launching out in new careers. With Robert Browning I say, "Grow old along with me, the best is yet to be."